Grieve

Stories and Poems
about Grief and Loss

Volume 9

Grieve Volume 9
Hunter Writers Centre
PO Box 494 The Junction
Newcastle NSW 2300

Email: publishing@hunterwriterscentre.org
Website: www.hunterwriterscentre.org

Grieve: *Stories and Poems about Grief and Loss*

ISBN-978-0-6488504-5-8

Cover design by HWC Publishing
Cover photo courtesy of Pexels and Philippe Donn
Typesetting by HWC Publishing
2021 Published by Hunter Writers Centre Inc.

sometimes loss makes possible a future

~ *What is Grief?* by Emily Noske

Awards

The National Association of Loss and Grief (NALAG)
I Don't Bring A Casserole - David Terelinck

The Pettigrew Family Funerals
What Is Grief - Emily Noske

The National Association of Loss and Grief (NALAG)
Minutiae - Sally Davies

In Memory of Terry Lynch
Writing a Heron, Writing of You - Kristen Roberts

Palliative Care NSW
Spelndour in Darkness - Polly Watkins

All About Grief
Dog Ears - J.M. Wildie

Lake Macquarie Memorial Park
Gold Lining - R I Quin

Newcastle Memorial Park
Mother - Celeste Alway

David Lloyd Funerals(Newcastle and Hunter Valley)
What We Learned from the Geisha Girl - Damen O'Brien

White Lady Funerals
Close, but ... - David Brewster

Simplicity Funerals
And Just Like That - Morna Seres

Interflora
Aubade for my Unborn - Kate Crowcroft

In Memory of Anthony Rappo
Lungs - Rosanna Diacci

The Calvary Mater Hospital Pastoral Care
Life Lessons - Emma Simpson

'Our World' Awards
Aftereffect - Jeanette Gellard
Fire and Ash: Autumn - Margret Lockwood

In Memory of Jan (Wendy) Wade
Birthday Song - Tahlia Dent

Mindframe
I Don't Want to Remember - Frankie Wright

The Blue Knot Foundation
Signs - Shari Kocher

The Compassionate Friends
A Prayer for Lost Dreams - Sally Eberhardt

In Memory of Richard A Andersson
Last Words - Kim Nolan

Hunter New England Health, Mental Health Services
She Is ... - Catherine Irvine

Hunter Writers Centre
Our Final Conversation - Tim Collins

Booktopia
Retrieving Gold - Jennifer Harrison

Good Grief
Intermission - Hanna Koskinen

I Don't Bring a Casserole

David Terelinck

I know how many friends will have come, filled your fridge with food which you are too tired to eat. I don't bring flowers; your living room will resemble a florist shop. I don't bring any condoling words. I know there are none that can help. I do take your favourite pair of dress shoes from the closet. I take the tin of Kiwi polish, the soft cloths, the antique horsehair brushes, and sit on your back verandah steps. I pick up the left Ferragamo first, pull the laces carefully through the eyelets. With a just-damp cloth I gently wipe away a fine layer of dust. I pop the top on the tin. I drag one end of the stiff-bristled brush through polish dark and pungent as grief. My left hand is mittened by the soft calf skin leather. With my right I start softly brushing, small circular motions, medium pressure, until the polish is evenly applied.

As I let the polish dry, I recall your story of these shoes. You were in Verona; had just visited Casa di Giulietta. You both brushed your hands against her bronzed breast for luck. Then you turned a corner, and there they were. Handmade. Leather uppers and soles. You tried them on and loved them. But you shied away from the price. Later, she returned and bought them for you. Always you saved wearing them for special occasions. Anniversaries. Birthdays. Ballroom dances. Dinners out with her.

I pick up the shoe, use the soft-bristled brush to remove excess polish. Then I take the chamois, work it back and forth across the surface; buffing against the grain. Slowly at first, then faster and faster to work in the polish and bring out the patent shine. When the shoe mirrors my face, I place it upon the step and slowly repeat the ritual with the right.

I relace both shoes when done, return them to your closet. You will have need of them tomorrow. We both know she would have wanted you to wear them; to look your very best. You don't say thank you. I don't expect it. I remember a time I walked in your shoes; a time when someone polished mine, because words were never enough.

What Is Grief?

Emily Noske

In March this year, a character in a marvel television series said to another:

'But what is grief, if not love persevering?'[i], and the words went viral.

It made me think; if there are a lot of grieving people out there, then there must be a lot of love out there, too.

My dad died in January. Pancreatic cancer.

His whole life he suffered from severe mental illness. He was often very angry and sometimes difficult to love, but I always did and do, and that makes me think:

but what is *love*, if not perseverance?

I wonder how this logic applies to other kinds of grief. When we lose parts of ourselves—our identities, our bodies—does love for these past parts endure as well?

I think if it does then grief must equal love, equal perseverance, equal *hope.*

When I was diagnosed with Bipolar Disorder Type 1, after a psychotic episode at 23, I thought I had completely lost myself.

But maybe my grief guided me in identifying what it was that I had liked about myself before.

My family and friends (their love, persevering) reminded me that I was still whole.

Does healing come from enduring then, from remembering?

At 27, I was asked whether I wanted to keep my breasts or have them removed.

I had lost my hair, my eyebrows, my eyelashes, and was getting used to the idea that sometimes loss makes possible a future.

I'm told I won a battle but all I really did was persevere.

My body full of hope and love and grief.

I live overseas. I am surrounded by mountains and it's beautiful, but it's a different kind of beauty to Australia, and occasionally there's a longing for home that feels deep like sorrow.

I realise grief reflects who we are and what we value and is probably always teaching us something, if only we can bear to listen.

I recently read a poem in a Grieve anthology by a woman who lost her 34 year old daughter to breast cancer and it made me cry and cry.

I cried for her and her daughter, and for my dad, and for myself.

A mix of pain and gratitude and guilt.

I wanted to tell that women her daughter was so lucky to have her as a mother.

I wanted to bear witness to that tremendous display of love,

persevering.

[i] WandaVision Episode 8

Minutiae

Sally Davies

There are 43 bricks between the window and the door. They're a mottled brick. I think they have flecks of glass or something like that in them. I'm sure I once heard that look described as *Spanish moss* by someone. Or was it *French moss*? Was it even moss? I thought paint colour naming was bad. Imagine having to name bricks.

The minister just mispronounced his name. Classic. I'd written it phonetically for him too.

A strip of light illuminates the ceiling, growing ever larger as the afternoon rolls in.

There's that calming voice: 'He was an amazing man.'

Yes he was.

What's also amazing is how the hair on the woman in front of me manages to sit so perfectly. Each strand lies in place like it has been methodically positioned by an OCD hairbrush. Can hairbrushes have OCD? Can inanimate objects obsess about order?

The order of service clasped in my hand feels awkward. Uncomfortable even.

My shoes feel uncomfortable too. Every time I wear them I remember why I dislike them so much. I wish I'd remembered before I left the house and was a significant distance from a back up pair. I always fell for their appearance of propriety. Is it possible to get gangrene from too tight shoes?

I hope Grandad's shoes aren't too tight. I'd given them his favourite pair to put on but he never liked the laces done too tightly. The bows were always perfect, but never too tight. He said it made his feet swell. I should have insisted I put them on him. I wonder if it's too late to do anything about that? Probably.

The watch on the wrist of the person behind me is ticking. I suppose watches do tick but are they always this loud?

The music has started. Reflection time. I don't want to reflect. I've had a week of reflection. There are no tears left.

My pounding heart trumps the sound of the watch but not the music. Bring back the tick. Or a brass band. Does anyone have bagpipes? Anything to drown out this beautiful, classical piece that was his absolute favourite.

He used to play the record for me on loop on a Sunday afternoon. I'd lie on the lounge room floor, staring at the ceiling and letting the music wash over me.

The flowers on top of the casket wash over the sides.

Who wears a floral shirt to a funeral? I think it's Mabel. Typical.

Actually, why is the neighbour even here? Hang on, is it the neighbour? Or a cousin? Would any of my cousins wear pearls? Family gatherings need name tags.

The Minister is back. At least he pronounced his name correctly this time. He must have found my notes.

Everyone's saying amen. Is that it?

The curtain slowly closes across the front of the casket. He's gone.

We all stand. We all leave. Well, all but the piece of my heart that's just disappeared behind that curtain.

Writing a Heron, Writing of You

Kristen Roberts

A pale-smoke heron strides the shallows of the flooding,
its elegance at odds with its local counterparts
          – the corellas frenetic, magpies lumbering –
and I remember a last afternoon with you:

a stirring of rain,
a flurry of visitors, jackets held over their heads
as they dashed for their cars,
          – you know, a little wet never hurt anyone –
and the tea trolley clinking closer.

You rubbed arthritic swellings,
fingers worrying at your epithelial gloaming,
and told me of the lake that formed once after a long rain,
an umbilicus of fallow land
that swelled like popular fallacy,

                              and of the birds
that gathered on its wind-riffled flank,
each uncommon for the area
          but chastising the imperiousness of each other's claim,

                              and how you found them one morning
          as the flood's girth dwindled,
feasting on the tender plants of your cultivated perimeter,

and how you'd chased them,
barefoot, unbuttoned shirt flapping like wings
that couldn't save you when you tripped.

Your hands always found the joint
at this point of the story. The break was so cruel
it needed pinning, and when you returned from hospital
both birds and lake were gone.

They're necessary fictions,
these temporary bodies, you'd said
and I'm still unsure if you meant the lake
or your own corporeal decline.

I wondered at the time
what I could write to anchor you here, to keep you,
not knowing I could simply write of a heron
and here you'd be.

Splendour in Darkness

Polly Watkins

It was unbearable to let you go but by the time you left us, to be honest, all our hopes that you would recover had frayed into one ragged, desperate hope: that your suffering would end. That you would die.

We lived in your hospital room, sleeping on a mattress beside your bed. Sometimes we climbed in with you, hugging our bodies against yours, reshaping ourselves to fit around the medical tubes pumping drugs to numb your pain. As your body became clamped with heaviness, your breathing shallow, our love grew big in the room. We breathed in your hair, your skin, talked of your teasing smile and dark shining eyes. Eyes that said everything there ever was to say between a mother and her children.

You were no longer able to speak, eat, swallow or move, your heavy-lidded eyes gave no flicker. I tapped my thumb against yours, but you returned no telegraphic message like Dad had when he was dying. I leaned over and whispered in your ear that I would give you two years of my life if I could. Your brows puckered and you blinked, just long enough for me to catch a shimmer of your black mica eyes telling me that you would never agree. Never.

Your granddaughter arrived. Heavily pregnant with her first child, she was so excited to tell us she had just heard her baby's heart-beat. We felt our hearts rush with unexpected lightness. Such a strange sensation, to feel joy bursting inside the stultifying darkness that consumed us.

We knew that hearing was the last sense to go so after each of us told you how much we loved you, again and again, your granddaughter began to sing. When she finished the last refrain and the air stilled, you gave us one last gift. Even as your heart faltered, you pushed your hand from under the bed covers and spread your shaky, knotted fingers across the span of her belly. Your face softened as you welcomed your first great grandchild, feeling her lusty kick, as you were preparing to leave.

A few hours after your death, the Eta Aquarids meteor shower peaked, lighting up the sky with shooting stars. It gave us a way to mark your splendour. You, who insisted on no funeral, just a simple cremation without fuss.

Gold Lining

R I Quin

Five minutes past six.

You wake. The eastern horizon is strung out in orange and pink, the sky clear, the air cool. The day has arrived. You never thought it would, yet time has flitted by, butterfly-erratic. They are all there, the people you love. They help you dress and do your hair. Flash your face in a mirror. You're told not to smile when they apply lipstick, but you can't help it. You stand before the mirror and see another girl reflected back. A beauty in white lace.

Five minutes past six.

You open your eyes in your solitary bed. It's dark. Clouds hang low and a fine mist-rain settles in the air. This day has arrived and you want to keep your eyes closed, open them when it's over. But time lumbers forward on elephant-legs. They will begin to gather: family, friends, people you have not seen in years. They will hug you and cry and you will be the one to comfort them. You dress, avoid the mirror, knowing the woman you will see is different to the one you feel inside.

Twenty minutes past three.

You stand at the end of the aisle, everyone you know seated in rows, but you are aware of none of them. Light streams through high windows, casting the room in gold. You feel nervous, happy. You see him standing at the altar, waiting for you. You see past him to the life you and he will share. You will leave here a wife and he a husband, changed by the day. Everything you have been till now will be described as *before*. Everything you will be from now on, described as *after*.

Twenty minutes past three.

You hear them behind you. Soft, respectful voices. The day remains grey, but the rain has stopped. They've covered the raw earth in green cloth. You wish they'd kept it as it was, red and rich. Dirt. No pretence. You feel nothing. You stare across the chasm of years at the young girl you were and you don't recognise her. She's gone and you are in her place. The clouds part for an instant. Sun shines through a crack in the clouds, creating a gold lining around the lid of the coffin. It's lowered down. The light disappears. Time stands still. You can't comprehend how deep this hole can be.

Dog Ears

J.M. Wildie

Nothing used to annoy me more than how my little brother, Albi, treated our books. Not his. Ours. While I strived to maintain novels like pristine artifacts, Albi attacked and inhabited them, leaving his mark in every volume he encountered. The number of times I'd take a novel from the bookshelf in our room only to find ten, twenty, sometimes fifty dog-eared pages, enough to distort the shape of the entire book. When I suggested a bookmark, he'd just shrug. Then there was his habit of scribbling his musings in the margins, pointing out flaws in the book's plot. At least once a week, we'd argue about Albi's vandalism. The conversation would eventually become about the content of the notes and we'd be up late into the night, discussing stories in depth, the initial dispute long forgotten.

At age thirteen, Albi got struck by a car. We spent the next week in the hospital, praying for the coma to end. On the third day, I brought along his favourite novels for him when he woke up. The following Saturday, the books came home unopened, left for me to place back on my bookshelf in my bedroom. Not ours. Mine.

The first time Albi or I had worn suits was at his funeral. He looked as unnatural as I felt. The eulogy was long, but I didn't recognise the boy my uncle was describing. Albi had become simplified, a caricature of himself. All rough edges sanded away for crowd-pleasing effect. Along with the heat, the well-wishers and condolences were suffocating. Back home, I did what came naturally when I felt lost. I picked up a book.

It was only a few pages in when Albi's first note appeared. He was being pedantic about an author not following their established time-travel rules, destroying any suspension of disbelief for me. On another page, he'd underlined a passage and simply wrote 'Wow' beside it. For the first time, I realised the dog-eared pages matched up with the best parts of the novel. There weren't enough bookmarks to keep track of everything Albi loved. I kept searching books for signs of Albi, persisting through the tears that dampened the pages.

After several books, I realised the finite nature of Albi's notes. There were only so many to discover. After stacking the novels back on the shelf by author, alphabetically, I chose one of my favourites. On the title page, Albi had written notes about his problems with the ending. A laugh cracked through, damp and haggard. I vowed to discover Albi's work the way it was intended. I had to read the books beginning to end, stumbling across Albi's intrusions along the way, never knowing which note would be the last. What I craved were those moments I read his messy handwriting and felt fourteen again. Feeling like I'd look up and see Albi dog-earing a favourite page before reading on. The room would feel like it was ours. Not mine. Ours.

Mother

Celeste Alway

I missed you most deeply when I was pregnant with my firstborn. A daughter. You'd said that our family was only cut out for quiet and bookish little girls. You were right. There were two more. Three daughters. Same as you. This is where the similarities end.

Each time, as my belly stretched beyond recognition, week by week, month by month, my heart was longing for the reassurances of my own mother. But I don't know if you were capable of such platitudes. You left twenty years before. Not by tragic circumstance but by choice. Oh, the horror.

What mother leaves her children and moves to the other side of the world? This is a good question. One that people ask all the time now that I am grown. But then, at the time, no one was asking anything at all. They weren't asking me, anyway. I was 12. My sister just 8. We were left to languish with our father. All of us depressed. We drifted around in our sad, little, dark house. What a horrible house. It wasn't a home. Is this why you had to go??

In the end, I came through it all ok. Career. Marriage. Children. Tick. Tick. Tick. Full points for conventionality. Dad found a new partner who adores him. She's turned him around. He's developed core family values. Wants to see me. My kids. We get along. It's better than it was. No doubt.

But my sister, she isn't as strong. She was so young. She's never recovered. In her teens and twenties, she ran the gauntlet of mental health disorders. Depression. Anorexia. Suicidal ideation. Self-harm. Now, she is older and has settled down, but lives alone. In the past. Ruminating over everything. Now she's keen to dig up our family history tree for a better understanding. I hope she gets the answers she needs. She has a career as a practicing psychologist, working with traumatised and deeply disturbed children. Naturally.

I thought of you endlessly as I cradled my babies. I was a new mother and all I wanted was my own mother to come and care for me. To tell me it would all be fine. That babies cried. That I wouldn't always be tired. That this phase would pass, just like the others. To prepare meals when I couldn't. To wash the endless laundry pile because I shouldn't. To hold the unsettled baby and play with the toddler so that I could leave the room and just breathe.

I had you for twelve years but, back then, I thought what we had was for life. Maybe this was selfish. Who said that mothers were forever? Perhaps some are only meant for a season.

I'm 42 now and I've spent three decades grieving. I think it's time to give it a rest. My own children need me so much now. They're 11, 6 and 4. Their father has met someone younger. Someone blonder. He's left.

What We Learned from the Geisha Girl

Damen O'Brien

We were cutting the hedge of Geisha Girl that some
fool had planted in a purple line on the North East side
of our hot house, though everyone knows that the
Geisha Girl can't be killed, you can poison or cut it
or dig out its roots and after a season it will be back,
its giraffe branches straggling, its heavy produce
of bitter orange berries that nothing enjoys, native birds
won't touch it, when you went in to answer the phone
and returned with news that your cousin's cancer,
caught in her lymph nodes, cored from her at great
cost, has been found in her bones, a sore second rib,
bruised beyond healing. You came back with tears.
This time it is terminal. Because it had to be done, we
finished the hedge. Your new shears made short work
of the branches, its green selfishness, a garden saw
to gnaw at the larger knots. Still, it shouldn't be that easy.

Close, but ...

David Brewster

The closest I have come to parenthood,
this blastocyst in bloom is never mine
to hold. An awful name, like something plump
with pus not life. It's just a bunch of cells—
to view it any other way requires
confronting death two weeks from every birth.
The failure of a cycle sounds mechanical:
a faulty chain, my wonky broken balls.
Why are repairs not possible?

I am close to coming in a plastic vial;
a nurse outside shares gossip with a laugh.
Not the pennant for my reproductive
pedigree I'd hoped to hoist, but lovemaking's
eyes strayed: the passion of a diary date,
then open liaisons with specialists.
I hand my worth's small measure over to her;
it sits unhappily on paperwork.
Why need this be dehumanising?

As close as I will never come to teaching
football in the winter sun. Or being called
that palindrome. Or holding hands across a road.
What's the point? Someone standing at a stone
remembering a mediocre man
they might have loved. Who knows. At least they'd feel
I'd had a go and given it my all—sweat
of the brow will raise the generations.
But it cannot help create them.

And Just Like That

Morna Seres

My father was a big man, capable of cramping almost everything around him. It would be quite impossible for me to tie up the four sides of a handkerchief in a neat pouch and say, *that is him, that is my father.* He would have oozed over the top, slid down the sides, gnawed at the fabric until it was torn open, refusing to be contained in some sort of neat appraisal. In a sense, I don't even think of him as something human. It is more to do with the texture of heat, like shifting volcanic lava broken down into fragments—hazardous, dynamic, brilliant, even incandescent, capable at times of transforming into something cold and hard.

When he was eighty-one, he left us.

My sister called me late on a Friday afternoon.

'You need to come,' she said.

I jumped in the car and drove the two hours it took me to reach my parents' house in the Blue Mountains. I was unprepared for what I saw. He was achingly thin, skin pulled across the bones of his face like ancient parched paper, threatening to fray or tear at any moment. I sat beside the bed positioned in the lounge room and held his hand. His wretched face, collapsing at the neck, contorted itself into a smile.

'My big beautiful girl,' he murmured between wispy cotton filled breaths.

My other sister arrived and the four of us remained on either side of him, keeping a bedside vigil throughout the night and into the next day. In between his laboured breathing, he muttered, while we swirled ice around the inside of his mouth. As the night wore on, he moved further away from us until the only thing we could hear was the rattle of death.

Towards dawn, my head resting on my father's bed, I heard my mother say, 'It's enough.'

Unsure what she meant, I watched anxiously as my middle sister left the room. She came back carrying a bottle of morphine and a syringe. Confidently, she sucked the drug through the needle and injected our sunken, dying father with the opiate. He disappeared bit by bit until, late in the afternoon, he passively and silently deserted us.

I felt a seismic shift, the tremor of the earth's crust redeploying itself to another position, forever altered. But it wasn't the violent, tearing shift of an earth in turmoil. It was a gentle wave, a subtle and heart-wrenching movement, and with it, a recognition the world was not as it had been. I rattled my memory, unleashing my father. A torrent of images raced past me: his arms reaching out to catch me off the swing, reading Cyrano de Bergerac to me in his Richard Burton voice, jitterbugging with my mother in the lounge room, holding me when I discovered my husband's affair.

And I struggled; struggled hopelessly in that sorrowful moment to understand the meaning of it all.

Aubade for my Unborn

Kate Crowcroft

How the sun's deep yolk
bled through I do not know—I'd fastened
the blackout curtain, latched its thick rope
along the window's throat, the twisted weight
a glottal clot in mine. Like all hungry things we lie

suspended in a morning's worth
of light; the hour when shadows
throw their people, take leave of night—
having given the earth and earth
now given. Nothing keeps

but hopes here, open
along a fault line. With my tongue, I tell him
the seed of 'chink' is *keim*

fissure, narrow valley, to cut meat
along the spine, from the Gothic through the Saxon
for *germinate* (the connection being in the notion
of bursting open.) In the golden hue that came

he traced
each vertebrae of the buried
town beneath my skin, pressed an ear
down the marbled vein, and listened
for the bodies
we might have made
and killed
in making.

Lungs

Rosanna Diacci

I know how to listen to lungs. I know how to read a chart. I know that today is Tuesday. I know that today is your fourth birthday. And I know that today is one week since we palliated you. I also know that I'm supposed to be objective. I'm your doctor, or at least I'm the student who's trying to be. So I listen to your lungs and I listen for the creps I know are there. And for my own sake I transform you from a child with an imagination and ideas and play into a set of symptoms and a set of blood results. And I try not think about how those lungs are so little. And I try not to think about how no one on your team actually knows how you're still alive. Your marrow is making blasts, and your T cells are on fire. And when your mum asks about your neutrophils, I have to tell her they're zero. They're still fucking zero. And they have been for weeks. And I know there's nothing we can do to pull them up. Everyone in this room knows that. Everyone knows how this ends. Everyone but you. You don't know it yet. Because you're four. And you don't understand why your blood is acid, or why there's a tube in your nose, or why we're pumping you full of poison that really only seems to make you feel worse. You don't know that every day we look at your chart and we hold our breaths waiting to find an inevitable fever. A fever you won't fight off. A fever no antibiotic, or antipyretic, or fancy American drug trial will ever bring down. We stand in your room and we wait for the fever we know will kill you. And I don't know it yet, but we do find that fever. We find it Friday week. And I try to stay objective, but my voice shakes when I read it. And I don't know it yet, but a week later you'll die. And your lungs will stay little forever. I'm told, over and over, that one day we'll cure it. I don't know it yet, but when you die they'll say that a lot. They'll say that we learnt from you. That the trials we knew were never going to save you, those trials learnt from you. And now we're closer than ever before. Thanks to you, one day we'll cure it. And I know that's supposed to help me shift the heaviness that settled on my chest the Tuesday you turned four. But it doesn't. Because one day we'll cure it. But I know we won't cure it in time for you. And I know your lungs will stay little forever.

Life Lessons

Emma Simpson

Drip.
Drip.
Drip.

Luna listened to the leaking tap and spat her toothpaste into the sink. She wiped her mouth on a towel and waited for the next drip. And the next.

She remembered listening to the same sound with her dad. She remembered perching on the edge of the bath, still in her school uniform, her dad on the floor wedged between the toilet and the basin, a leaking tap between them. Her dad had interrupted her favourite TV show and she'd been annoyed.

'You've got to turn off the water at the mains first. It's the tap on the front lawn, the one I showed you last week. Remember, *righty tighty, lefty loosey.*'

Luna hmphed and strained to hear the TV but her dad's voice was too loud. Giving up, she considered the ends of her ponytail. She noticed a few split ends and pulled them out.

'Pumpkin, are you listening?' Luna lifted her eyes to find her dad staring at her.

'Yeah, sure Dad. Turn the water off first,' Luna mumbled.

'No.' She was surprised by the firmness of his voice. 'Remember to put the plug in. You don't want to drop anything down the sink.'

'Okay, OKAY,' Luna placated, dropping her hair.

Luna watched and listened as her dad showed her how to take off the tap cover, the little button with the 'C' printed in bold, then the skirt and spindle. She felt the phone in her pocket vibrate and took it out.

'Luna.' Her dad slammed the wrench on the bathmat beside his knee. 'Pay attention. This is important.'

'But it's not, Dad. If I need to fix a tap I'll just wait for you.'

Luna watched her dad considering what to say. 'What if I'm not here? You've got to be able to look after yourself.'

'If you're not around, Mum will call a plumber.' She thought the emotion in her dad's voice was a little over the top. 'It's just a tap, Dad. Relax.' She lowered her eyes to her phone and read the text.

'It's more than a bloody tap.' His words reverberated around the small room, his frustration bouncing off the tiles. 'It's about being capable and self-reliant. People won't always be around to help.' Luna heard the pause in his voice and looked up. 'It's about managing on your own.'

He bent his head and took a deep breath before rummaging in the toolbox and coming up with a packet of washers. 'And put that bloody phone away before I throw it away.' The tone of his voice left no room for negotiation and Luna did as she was told. She learnt how to fix a dripping tap.

Within the year he was gone.

If only she had listened better, asked more, then maybe she would've learned how to fix everything. Maybe she would've learned how to live without him.

Aftereffect

Jeanette Gellard

Before

I'm scared. Not the stomach dropping, fast heartbeat, kind of scared. More a sense of dread, disquiet, unease. Its stealthy approach is unsettling. It's been days now, perhaps even weeks. I hadn't really noticed, distracted by the everyday until I realised the everyday had shifted, just slightly. The catastrophic forecasts had begun.

Now

The fire is coming now. It's moving faster than I could imagine. I move around the house, checking once again my preparations. The house is in lock down. Outside objects cleared away or moved inside. Windows shut. Curtains open. Doors closed. Baths and sinks filled with water. Wet towels at the ready.

My body is covered by thick clothing, boots, a hat, gloves, face mask. I'm unrecognisable, even to myself.

There is a darkness to the daytime that shouldn't be. Thick smoke embraces me without affection. Heat that chills my core. All an affront to my senses.

In an otherwise quiet landscape, the fire is roaring. The wildlife has gone. Escaped or perished, I do not know.

The fire hose writhes in my hand. Saturating the ground, filling the gutters, wetting the walls. The sound of the pump lost in the wind racing in front of the fire. I'm breathing heavily from the effort.

I've moved inside. It arrives. It moves on. I move outside.

Sunlight seeps in, visibility is dull and hazy. Sounds emerge from what's left of the scrub. Creaking, crashing, the trees in the scrub still responding to the blaze that has passed. The taste of the now gone fire acrid in my mouth.

My house is still standing. So am I.

Later

I didn't feel it at first. The aftereffect. It was like sitting in hot bath water that goes cold over time. If I lie still everything is fine. If I move, the surface of the bath water is disturbed and touches my dry skin. It feels cold. How did it get so cold? I was warm and now I am shivering. Time to pull the plug, get out, reach for the towel.

My shivers are on the inside now. If I pull the plug what will drain away?

I'm scared.

Fire and Ash: Autumn

Margret Lockwood

The oaks have done it again
shaking their grey frames free
from the weight of gold.

A twelfth season of frost has come
to ice the grass,
to fringe again in lace
the fallen leaves in the village gutters.

These autumn afternoons
as kindling catches and soot dislodges
I recall how hope billowed
then grew thin as smoke
drifting over the avenue.

The oaks will green again,
shading the road by the fire station
where twelve springs ago
the red coffin passed
the yellow guard of honour.

Birthday Song

Tahlia Dent

My kui fefine, my grandmother, says that she has only ever fallen in love with two men: my sweet grandfather and Elvis Presley.

It's a Sunday morning in late May. My brothers and I gather with my mother in the dining room. The smell of rain slips through our open front door and the sound of tree branches tossing in the wind harmonises with the phone ringing out.

She answers.

And we all start talking and yelling at the same time, our well wishes climbing and falling all over each other. I tell her that for her 70th birthday, I have learnt to play her favourite song on the piano.

I linger on the first chord and it sounds like the melody of a Tongan morning peeling into the day like the blue paint of their house. Church bells ringing, the kettle whistling and the soft hum of my Grandfather reading. After the third note, kui fefine is already singing the melody.

Wise men say …

It sounds like her and him. Like the time they accidentally left me a voicemail of the two of them singing 'Blue Suede Shoes' in the car. Him and her. Sometimes I dream of them singing that song. I dream of it from start to finish.

Like a river flows, surely to the sea …

We can hear a shuffling sound like the phone is moving. Kui fefine keeps singing and it sounds like she is dancing—on mats woven long before us, her feet scuffing and scraping like soft waves.

'Play louder,' she says.

So I do.

For I can't help falling in love with …

Her voice trails off.

I've stopped playing now. My mother and my aunt have folded into each other, fallen back into the lounge. Both panting and laughing. I can hear Grandma dancing, still.

I imagine that her eyes are closed and her face is wet. That she holds her arms up, one falling to rest on his shoulder, and the other in his hand. She slowly turns, and I can see a faint glow behind her coming from a soft chorus of open windows and streaked sunlight. When she stops and looks back to me her face is dry and her arms by her side; her shadow stands alone against the wall.

I hear her smile through the phone and she says, 'You play just like he did.'

I want to say to her, *I know you hear him in everything. Some days, I do too.*

I want to close the piano, tuck in the stool, climb the distance between us and move quietly towards her. I'd let my palm brush her back before kissing her gently on the cheek—just like the hands and lips of her sweet husband—I'd whisper some words, words I'm sure he once would have said.

Ma'u ha 'aho fiefie. Ofa lahi atu.

But everyone yells goodbye together and before I can join in, the line falls silent.

Happy Birthday. I love you.

I Don't Want to Remember

Frankie Wright

Words seem to run into each other in my mind, like curling smoke. It feels like you are watching me. Waiting. Voiceless, bodiless, trapped in my memory in a place and time, your stories lie dormant entwined with my own. You lived, you breathed, you laughed, you hoped. Then it stopped.

I shake my head and close my eyes. Now, I see only your face. I don't want to see it. I don't want my last memory of you to be your small daughter holding your cold pale hand, whispering in your ear, her tears glistening in your hair. I don't want to remember giving the eulogy. I don't want to see myself stand in front of your family, watching their shifting masks threaten to come away under fresh waves of rage and grief. I don't want to hear their excuses for why you lived the way you lived, and why you died the way you died.

I don't want to see your father's cold hard eyes, or watch him skull another beer, crumple the tin, and shrug as if to say there was nothing more to be done. I don't want to remember lying in bed with you, when we were young, while your body was wracked with sobs as you told me the things your father said to you and begged for him to love you, while I stroked your hair and wished I could take the pain away.

I don't want to remember the last phone call, where you asked me question after question after question, about me and my life. At last, I asked how you were, and you were silent. Then you cried and hung up.

I don't want to remember when you told me what those boys did to you, and that I told no one, like you made me promise. Who was there to tell?

I don't want to see how gaunt you were, like you were trying to be invisible in life, but we all looked upon you in death. I don't want to see your mother take your face in her hands and tell us all she brought you into this world, and now she is sending you out of it.

I tried so hard to pretend I was somewhere else, but then I felt that tug on my skirt. Your daughter looked up at me, and I couldn't look away. 'were you my mother's friend?' she asked. Her intense blue eyes are the same shade as yours, but yours were closed in the final sleep. I nodded.

'I like your boots,' she said approvingly, and she took my hand. I squeezed it tight.

I don't know where you are now, I thought. But I swore I could hear you laughing, like you used to, when we were children.

Signs

Shari Kocher

Weather and seasons and their individual rooms, cardboard, clapboard, timber. My family had no friends, there really was no other body. No child companion, or pet, or interested party, but the wild kookaburra at my bedside, the cane toads I was taught to run from, the treefrogs pulsing at the window with their clear green bellies, more frightening in the dark, though not hostile, exactly. Not one human confidante in my first six years of life, unless you count the old ones. School a shock: so many other bodies, some almost my size. What did that sequestering my parents did from others, do to me? The teaching was: you don't need anyone. But I was ardent, hungry, made friends easily, lost them also the next day in groups of chatter. The imaginary with whom I conversed became the real music of water, of tree frogs, of dripping ferns, kookaburra glistening through wet season and dry, thunderstorms I learned to read as personal, passionate signs. Not the jets that rent the eardrums of the sky. No television, no radio, two isolated parents, one upstairs in a hot kitchen, one downstairs in a home office I was not to disturb. Nothing but those jets ever happened. No outings or visitors, nothing to break the tedium except the occasional camping trip that went awry. Floodwaters the car had to be winched through. Riverwater trashing the towel-tight doors. My father deciding to leave my baby brother on a corner in a strange town because he cried too much. The horror and fear and sickness of it. The way my mother said nothing. What that did to me too. The why of it comes clearer now. But not the recoil. How old wounds weep on certain days a clear liquid like the boil on the cat's paw the vet says is a good sign, although the cat is old and has cancer. Truly, I do not know what love is. Except upwards from the ground, and from stars whose creaturely eyes are not impersonal, or invisible, though these too I know. The truth is, I hardly ever think about that never lasting home hometown, even if town itself is an ambitious word, perched on the edge of wild brumbies pouring dense red darkness out ahead of fire.

A Prayer for Lost Dreams

Sally Eberhardt

I was blind-sided. I had no clue, no inkling this could happen to me.

I thought it was simple. You got pregnant; you had a baby. When it takes so many years for the first part to happen, you assume the second part automatically follows.

Of course, I'd heard of miscarriage, but it's like whiplash—never anticipated, and you have no idea how much it hurts until it happens to you.

I thought we were 'safe' now we were past the three-month mark.

I was wrong.

We expected to see precious new life at our twelve-week scan.

The nurse was quiet, then, in a soft voice, said she couldn't find a heartbeat. We asked her to keep looking, it had to be there. She whispered that our baby's heart was not beating. We asked her to repeat this a few times. We couldn't hear, then we couldn't believe what we were hearing.

My mother-in-law thought I was joking when I told her we lost the baby. She asked where it was. When realisation hit, she felt terrible and apologised profusely.

I know she didn't mean to hurt me.

My mother reminded me about the miscarriage she had when I was two years old. She said people consoled her by saying she already had a beautiful little girl, but she wanted *that* baby too. I bit my tongue and tasted resentment. What if this was my only chance at motherhood? She had three more children. I would give anything to have just one.

I know she didn't mean to hurt me.

Some people express their heartfelt sorrow for your loss, some say nothing because they don't know what to say. One old friend chose that time to tell me she was pregnant … again.

I know she didn't mean to hurt me, but we aren't close anymore.

Another friend, herself childless by choice, said it best—'I know you had so many hopes and dreams for this little one.'

That's it exactly. The hopes, the dreams, the anticipation, the overwhelming love you feel—where do they go? What do you do with them?

Grief is love with no place to go. Grief is a lost dream; a future that becomes a past instead of a reality.

They sent me home to decide if I wanted a procedure or to let nature take its course. I hate hospitals and chose nature.

We were driving when it happened. My waters burst on the seat and my husband pulled into the nearest servo. I hobbled to the loo, back aching and insides cramping.

They didn't tell me you experience labour. At least the physical pain takes your mind off your mental anguish.

Then, with a flush, that part of my life was over.

I will never stop at that servo again, but every time I pass by, I say a little prayer for lost dreams.

Last Words

Kim Nolan

Please do not put Linen in the cupboard. Thanks.
blu-tacked to the cupboard
across the corridor
from the room where my father labours for breath
the sign my eyes are compulsively re-reading

the hum of 9 litres of oxygen per minute
as I match my breaths to his
but can't sustain it without hyperventilating

the slightest of pressures from his fingers
in the hand that I hold
are what I know I will remember

the huh and sigh punctuation
of goodbye
most conversations with my dad were made up of silences between words

hungry and nauseated
between morphine naps he tells me
I had my tea!
You had your tea? When?
When I was asleep.
What did you have?
Tomato soup.
Was it nice?
Yeah.
Are you still hungry?
Nope.

She is ...

Catherine Irvine

She slowly crept towards me, silently in the dark. She knew I was not expecting her; I was busy, I was running from place to place, task to task, trying to live my life in the after.

She had been following me for some time, trying to let me know she was there, whispering in my ear. Had I heard her? Maybe. Did I want to listen to her? Not really. Maybe I had hoped that if I ignored her for long enough, she would go away this time.

Every season she comes, and every season she takes me by surprise. I never know when she will arrive, or when she will leave. I never know if she will creep in slowly and comfortably settle into my being, or whether she will burst through the front door with her mountains of baggage and turn my world upside down.

And she doesn't just come in the season, she watches and waits then chooses her moment to swoop down to try and envelop me in her darkness. She knows the moments that should have been, and she reminds me, taunts me, she wants to make me hurt.

As I walked him towards the classroom on the first day of school, there she stood … at the door of what would have been her classroom. Her harsh whispers travelled across the school grounds—*she should be here.*

She dragged my eyes across the playground, showing me the smiling children being ushered into their classrooms for the very first time.

'That should be you' she whispered, as my gaze fell on the proud mothers waving them off.

'Stop it,' I screamed, but nothing came out.

After five years I should know better. My season is here and with it comes her, yet I was not aware of her creeping slowly towards me, silently in the dark. She was standing right there beside me, but I did not see nor hear her. The pain arose from deep inside of me, cascading out of my body, washing over me and everything around me.

'It's time,' she whispered, and I knew that I needed to let her in.

They took my daughter and gave me her instead. I did not want her; I did not ask for her. I tried to fight but she found her place and settled in. I am the only one who sees her, I am the only one who hears her, she is a part of me, and she will never leave me. She only exists because my daughter did.

She is … grief.

Our Final Conversation

Tim Collins

I watch a young butcherbird
clamped to the gutter, it is
dun-coloured and awkward,

what goes through its head
at the edge of a hospital roof,
does it swallow hard, pushing

fear to the upside of its beak as
it shakily launches itself onto
air currents, flying nervously?

Dad shuffles from the toilet saying,
"most days it bulldog clips itself
to the gutter then just shunts off."

I walk from his room after our
goodbyes and he wryly touts,
"get bulldog clip in a poem son."

Retrieving Gold

Jennifer Harrison

after Eavan Boland's 'Requiem for a Personal Friend'

For the entire year after you died, I stepped over
your imagined presence by the side of my bed.
You slept there every night for fifteen years
and now my morning routine remembers
you for another twelve months:
the ritual of your waiting for me to wake,
then on old arthritic legs you'd struggle to your feet
and follow me down the hall or to the bathroom door
wherever. Then you would wait in the nearest door space
so that I would have to step over you again
on my way somewhere else. I imagine what
animal psychologists would make of this dance
of attachment and devotion—but they would not
understand the companionship of our language,
the dictionary of our spaces, the way after the final seizure
I held your paws and your old eyes looked
peacefully into mine as the sweet drug
mellowed your pain and I stepped with
you across the divide, your tongue's ghost by my side.

Intermission

Hannah Koskinen

Jase was last seen by a CCTV camera at 5.44pm walking through Cowan Station. He would often cross the motorway overpass beside the station, casually limbering up above six lanes of incessant droning before slipping into the bush on the other side, where the commuter roar would gradually give way to an intense quiet broken only by his breathing, his footsteps, and his thoughts.

Despite the best efforts of numerous men and women with impressive and curtailed credentials like Det and Insp, Jase has been missing for nearly three years. I am grateful for their work, but this is truly a tough slog, this perennial uncertainty. I don't know if his disappearance was his own choice, or accidental, or something cold and sinister. Crucially, I don't know if I will ever know.

Occasionally, I look through the hundreds of faces in the national register of missing persons, and it is the most sobering experience anybody can have. I'm not sure why I do this, but I suppose it gives me some solace to know that there are other families out there living in the same loose limbo. Jase is in there, of course, in the register. I wonder how many people click on his photo and read the bare facts of his case, like the blurb of a mystery novel, only to hit the back button once their passing curiosity has been sated.

Our son asks about Daddy sometimes, wanting him to come home and read a book, or race toy cars, or simply share a close embrace. He is four now. His relationship with Jase has been mostly formed from photos and stories, but I really hope he has some genuine memories locked away in that clever mind. I have had to face realities and tell him that Daddy may not ever return. The lack of finality clouds his understanding: *So Daddy might come home one day? Can we go and see him?* His questions are the same as mine, and they go similarly unanswered.

Jase's disappearance is grief by thousands of small cuts, subtly inflicted, one for each day that he doesn't walk through the front door. It is loss without closure, an unfinished chapter to a living biography. It is the pain of realising that perhaps there are answers to all my questions, and somebody is withholding them.

I will carry on, because amongst the despair there will always be hope. My best hope right now is that I can one day give this chapter of Jase's book the conclusion that it deserves.

Previous editions of
Grieve
are available to purchase as
paperbacks or downloadable ebooks from
grieveproject.org

Winter paddle-out at Cabarita Beach

Tony Lintermans

In the park above the beach they struggle
into wetsuits, like raw painters unsure
how lumpy memories fit a practised scene
then straggle shoreward, lugging boards.
The unforgetting brother hoists
the hessian bag with its plastic box of ashes
and starts the paddle to Nobbies Point, where
Jordan once dazzled on teenage waves.
A dozen others follow, past local surfers
catching what they can on what for them
is a small day. Before the circle forms
with linked hands and bobbing boards, the mother
is in the sea, wading against the swell,
wanting to be closer one last time.
Friends and family waiting on the beach
or watching from the cliff top cannot hear
the goodbyes spoken or see the ashes tumble,
at last the lucid drift through green-lit sea.
A life refracted shimmers, and shoals away.
At the pub for lunch, we share a fragile cheer.
The breaking surf just audible, like grief.
If the sea in Jordan did him in —
too big, too scary, years of rearing voices
jammed in the jar of my head,
no-one can ride these freight trains home —
the sea eventually took him in.
Afterwards, I think of Jordan on that beach
and how the deep library of the sea
keeps sending its riddles sideways, in waves
angling around the point towards us
to break in scribbles of ribboned foam
decodable only with patience.
I think of the mother who waded, and waited
so lovingly, and what she reads.

The Great Ocean Road, January last

Susan Bradley Smith

At Lorne: police policing the dawn road alive with ocean dew and blood. There is no way through for you. A bus, a car full of teenage girls, the wrong kind of hit and kiss, no way out but up to the crying sky. The rescue helicopters carry the almost dead and their witnesses angel-fast back to Melbourne's hospitals. Who's saving who here I wonder, turning inland as instructed, the only route left opened. Country towns zoom in on me with their soft focus. I am not crying, they are not my children, I don't know anyone here, I have enough petrol in my tank to drive past all roadkill to Mumbai, I'm just waiting for the highway to build itself. Over my shoulder (left) the ocean begs for my return and (right) crazed survivors from a bush doof stumble from the stringybarks. I was tempted to buy a tractor at Colac, I was tempted to buy wine at Tilly's vineyard, and muffins in the village of women wearing peasant dresses, but the act of purchase had lost its tranquilising effect. Those girls were dead. It was being broadcast already, screened. I was road-tripping with my daughter the metallic sun-orchid and this time we had no surfboards or dogs and those girls of the early morn were even longer dead by the time we looped back to the thin coastal road and reached the Southern Ocean Villas at Port Campbell where we always stayed but of which she had no recall. But I have proof. I have a photo of us taken by the nanny it is a picture of a father and a mother and five children attached to our limbs like mutations, behind us is water fresh from cold Antarctica with much to moan about and the famous rocks they call the Apostles who likewise vibrate with news but I am even deafer now than I was then and have nothing worthy to pass on. This impossible road was built by hopeful people swap those adjectives and you have the truth, there's a holiday snap for you.

Grieve

Ana Louisa Davis

I wanted to slip into bed with your cold body,
drape my long hair on your funny pigeon chest—
create a palm tattoo that would be buried with you.

I wanted to press my breasts against the taut curve of your back,
stroke the strange raised whorl of your belly button—
a birth-scar that had never healed.

I wanted to uncurl your bony fists
and rest my hands inside
like quiet shells.

I wanted to wrap my hands around your tight grip—
one final *paper over rock.*

Missing

Brenda Proudfoot

A figure walks past the distant eye
of a security camera. A father,
an elder wandering, lost in dementia.
A misper in blue shirt, grey pants, black shoes,
a stranger's face in a family snap.

I think of you as I pass a searched
remnant of spotted gum and ironbark forest
between Lakelands and Macquarie Road.
On the verge, a swathe of white lilies,
their alien bulbs rooted in ancient soil.

Five months now have passed since
you went missing near Lake Macquarie,
Awaba, the lagoon where men once fished
from bark canoes, backlit by smouldering fires.
Have you found your final resting place?
Are you lost, here, where you belong?

Let's Pretend

Pippa Kay

There's a creature with bad spit on the other side of our bedroom door. It's black and scaley. It waddles like a duck, and you'll burn if its spit lands on you. My brother Danny and I have our backs against the door to keep it out; our legs are propped on the floor, our heels digging into the lino.

We're at our Gran's house, and we both know the monster isn't true. It's one of our pretend games.

Gran knocks on the door.

'What's the password?' I ask.

'Chocolate crackles.' When we open the door, she slips in quickly, before the monster. 'Into bed you two.'

'Can we make chocolate crackles tomorrow?' asks Danny.

'If you're very good,' she says. 'All night long.'

It's not fair, because Danny's too young to be good all night long. He cries for Mummy and Gran has to tuck him in again. I used to cry too but I don't now. I'm older.

Gran tucks us in so tightly the mattress curves like a boat and she rocks it side to side. When she thinks we're asleep she turns off the light and tiptoes out, half-closing the door behind her.

Soon, Danny is crying. I get out of my bed and go over to him.

'Shh,' I say, 'or we won't make chocolate crackles tomorrow.'

'B-b-but, I miss Mummy.'

'I've got a secret,' I say. 'I'm not really your sister, I'm our Mummy.' I tuck him into his bed again and rock the mattress. 'When Mummy died I breathed her in, so I could be her.'

'How come she hasn't gone to heaven?' he asks.

'Heaven's only for daytime,' I say. 'She comes back to earth and visits at night.'

'Like a ghost?'

'Sort of. But not so scary.'

'Does she visit Gran too?'

'No, so we won't tell. She might not think it's fair.'

He nods, wipes his eyes on his pyjama sleeve. 'What colour is heaven?' he asks.

I climb back into my bed. 'Blue, like the sky.'

'Does everyone have their own cloud?'

That's a tricky one. 'Only if you want one,' I say. I close my eyes and imagine heaven, even though I know it's just pretend. There'll be more questions in the morning. One thing I know for sure is that they only have chocolate crackles in heaven. No cabbage.

'Are you still …?' he asks when we sit down to breakfast.

'Shh,' I say, as Gran pours honey on his porridge.

After breakfast we make chocolate crackles. Gran melts the copha, I sift the cocoa and icing sugar into a bowl on top of the rice bubbles. Danny stirs.

When we feed the chooks for Gran, Danny asks: 'What does God look like?'

'I'm me again now,' I explain. 'I don't know. We'll ask Mummy tonight.'

'Okay.' He smiles.

'Did you bring a chocolate crackle for the creature with bad spit?' I ask.

We'll keep playing these games. They stop his tears.

hey Prue

Mark Bromhead

hey Prue,
do you know they placed a red grevillia behind your ear and applied make-up to your face shortly after you died?
where did they think you were going? to a party?
i guess the nursing staff wanted you to look pretty in death for your eleven year old daughter's sake.
you looked nice,
but it didn't look like you.
i joined the family huddle around your bed and studied a stain on the hospital wall.
our father said: she's up there with mum. in a better place.
are you? up there, i mean, in a better place.

hey Prue,
do you know your hearse was covered with frangipanis?
—the yellowy ones and the pinkish ones.
during the service the funeral celebrant called them carnations.
we all looked at each other and lip-synched: 'carnations?'
when it was over, everyone trooped out of the chapel,
to the musical accompaniment of monty python's always look on the bright side of life.
it was your idea, your husband said,
because you thought it might be a pleasant way to ease the sorrow and grief.
you were wrong.
i used to like that song.

hey Prue,

do you know i didn't attend your cremation?
two funeral services for you in one day would have been overkill.
i hope you still laugh at your big brother's sarcasm.
afterwards, i received advice from kind-hearted souls: time heals all wounds.
no, it doesn't.
: it might make you feel better if you remind yourself she'll forever be forty-seven.
no, it doesn't.
: thinking of the good times you shared will help.
no, it doesn't. it doesn't.

hey Prue,

do you know if you google the word grieve
you get sixty five million nine hundred thousand results in half a second?
i better get started.

Louise

Jennie Keenan

You came into my bedroom and sat next to me on the bed. You didn't need to knock ... I always left the door open a crack.

'I'm a bit worried about you,' You said to me in a hushed voice, in the motherly tone You'd been honing for years. 'I think ... that we should talk about contraception?'

It all rushed out of me then, those teenage emotions too extreme to hold at bay for long.

'It's too late for that,' I wailed, hunched over my knees.

When I look back on it now, so many years later, I still feel completely overwhelmed. A hazy fog distorts it all, my memories unreliable, the feelings unresolved.

You held me as we sat on my bed. I felt such shame. I'd let You down. I'd disappointed You. It was the worst conceivable thing.

You took the day off work, and drove me to the doctors. I don't remember how far along I was. All I remember was that they made me wait until I was sixteen weeks.

'Why do we have to wait so long?' You had demanded.

I don't remember the answer. It doesn't seem so important now. The day of the appointment comes to me like a faded dream. We spent all day at the hospital, waiting. Waiting. Waiting.

We drove past protestors out the front. Holding signs and yelling bible verse. You squeezed my knee, didn't say a word.

I was cold lying on the stretcher. You rubbed my arms to warm me up.

You held my hand to keep me focused. You stayed by my side.

I remember feeling lucky. There were other girls in the waiting room. Other women. So many of them were alone. But I had You. I always have You.

When I woke up, all I heard was Your voice. Strong. Commanding.

'How is she? Let me go sit with her.' Of course they let You, there was no room for debate.

A cool hand in mine. Linked arms as we walked back to the car.

The memories are hazy now. It's been so long, and I try not to think about those years. I shove them down deep where they can't hurt me, where I let them fester silently.

What I do remember is You. That constant support. That endless love.

Now, You're fading. I see it happening every day. An enduring force, shrinking from within, with no way to help You. A cool hand clasped in Yours, linked arms as we walk together. I grieve the loss of You well before it's even happened.

I try to think that I will be okay when You're gone. But we both know that Your absence will leave an indelible mark. You've been through this too. You know how it feels.

I go into Your bedroom, and sit on an empty bed. I don't need to knock, You always leave the door open.

Living Grief

Margaret Conley

My blood ran cold when I heard tyres screech on the nearby main road. I dropped the spoon I was stirring the soup with and ran out the front door. Prostrate on the road was my 6-year-old-daughter. Remote control took me over as I entered the ambulance with my unconscious little one.

The flying doctor bore us to the Royal Children's Hospital in Melbourne, 300 kilometres away. Still in the sky, my daughter received a blood transfusion. Her system rejected the blood type and she almost died.

In the Intensive Care Unit, I was told her brain had bounced around inside her skull and there was massive bleeding. On my return to ICU after this diagnosis, the nursing staff ran to meet me. My daughter was almost brain dead. She was in a coma but her vital signs registered my absence. Again, she almost died.

Together, we spent fifteen gruelling weeks in the Children's Hospital. The plane banked to land at Albury on our way home; it dropped in altitude. Laughter broke from my daughter's lips, her first sound. My joyous daughter was there inside this still little person. The bright, energetic, fun-loving 6-year-old who ran out the door to buy an ice cream fifteen short weeks ago would never return. This fragile little being needed all the love my family and I could give her. In assisting her to wellness, she inspired me and tethered me to reality.

My daughter's determination to live against heavy odds is like a plant pushing through the parched, cracked earth in time of drought. Coma arousal therapy, the rain and sunshine that nourished her, was given by a dedicated team of 100 volunteers each month. Generous applications of love broke through the damaged soil of a vegetative state.

Medical intervention, exercise physiology, and hydrotherapy maintain her limited muscular control. Community access to cafes, cinemas, musical events and drama keep her brain active and give her emotional support. She is totally dependent on others for every detail of daily living. Everyone who meets her is touched by her determination to live. Her healing is slow but continuing. It is not uncommon for us to be surprised by the utterance of an unexpected word, or to see how she reacts to impulsive actions toward her by her peers—a high five, or 'knuckles' greeting. She exudes an aura of love. Just by being her, she brings joy into the hearts of those who spend time with her, and empowers them to live life more fully.

The mantra I used in the early days for my daughter was, 'You are getting better, in every way, every day'. These words worked their magic in both directions. Together we became 'better' people. Thirty five years later, we still have days of sunshine and days of rain but they make the rainbow that is our life together. Living with grief has given me the best version of myself.

Maybe We Should Just Have a Baby

Jack Hutchison

Christina and I were in bed when I said, 'Maybe we should just have a baby.'

A fly was buzzing between us, so I turned on the light to swat it with an orange Penguin I'd been meaning to read.

'It might help,' I said.

Christina was crying. She said to me, 'You know I want to.' Then she goes, 'But I'm sick of you saying that whenever we fight.'

'I mean it,' I say to her. 'I want you to stop taking your pill tomorrow.'

'Daniel,' she says. 'Don't.'

I tell her, 'I'll throw them out myself if I have to.'

Then I climbed back into bed, held her very tightly, and said, 'I'm serious.'

'OK,' she said. 'I love you so much.'

It was similar to how we decided to get married. ANZAC Day of 2013, just shy of two years earlier. We'd negotiated our way home through a foggy Hyde Park dawn service. The veterans didn't seem to take much notice of us but the families, the common conscientious folk, looked appalled. You don't forget faces like those.

Christina waited until we were under the covers then said, 'You were talking to Stephanie a lot tonight.'

I said to her, 'And?'

'And how do you think that makes me feel?' she says. 'Watching you all jokey with someone who you used to sleep with?'

I say, 'This incessant jealousy is wearing me out, Christina.'

'You're not emotionally superior, Daniel,' she says. 'You're not above jealousy.'

I ask her, 'Have I ever gone through your phone while you were sick in the bathroom?'

'I've never given you a reason to,' she tells me. 'You are always on your phone. Every time I look I find something.'

With a raised voice I say, 'Are you going to torture me forever over that?'

I contemplated the sincerity of my outrage, then added, 'I don't know how much longer I can keep doing this.'

Christina curled up and started howling.

It took her a minute to get out, 'Don't leave me.'

Then I held her and said, 'I think we should get married.'

Christina's invited me to our daughter's fifth birthday party this weekend. I've bought her a jewellery craft kit 'cause she hardly looks up from her iPad. Her hair hangs beside little golden coins, flashing red lights, jumping blocky villagers. I figured something tangible would be good for her.

One time I confronted Christina about the issue. I said, 'She spends too much time on that thing.'

'Don't lecture me, Daniel,' she said. 'You only have her once a fortnight.'

'It can't be good for her,' I say. 'She doesn't look me in the eye.'

'Your eye contact isn't great either,' she says. 'She'll need to use it at school next year.'

I say, 'I don't want her to be like me.'

'What? A coward?' Christina chuckles. 'Sorry, Dan. That was harsh.'

I said, 'It was basically what I meant.'

A Hunting Dreamtime-Grievetime Ceremony

Mark Lock

I remember looking forward to the camping trips to Mudgee with dad and two brothers. I was a fourteen-year-old 'Bull' as my step-dad affectionately tagged me. At the farm outside Narromine, I had busy dreams where I packed my camping bag with boots and polish, rifle and bullets, jeans and warm clothes, skinning knife and sharpening stone, and chocolate. The school holidays came, and I remember watching dad's Holden V8 sedan bump along the dusty track, giving mum a big hug goodbye, checking my gear, and sitting in the youngest sibling seat for the long drive to a far-away hunting vacation.

The joy of country smells! The car window opened enough to let out dad's cigarette smoke, but the wonderful eucalypt smell seeped-in as the day warmed. I loved the smell of a hot gun muzzle if I shot a kangaroo in the dusk. Success meant the iron taste of warm 'roo blood on my hands. The smell of a fresh skun animal was a mixture of cut fur, punctured stomach gas, scuffed-up dust, and boy hormone sweat. A good start to the trip, this ritual, as I salted and rolled up the skin.

I gave no thoughts to that ritual as a young, unreflective boy. Only the twisting and turning dirt roads and many cattle grids occupied my bouncing bladder. I was excited to arrive at the rusty tin and weatherboard family house on the property outside Mudgee. I loved the dirt-dry squeal of drum brakes, the squeaking of my boots as I ran to open gates, the magpies calling out from the wire, the thumping pump of the car's engine, the excited chatter of my brothers, and of Slim Dusty playing through the stereo cassette (ABBA came in later years).

To the relatives, a long hello was necessary before hunting talk—which creek to start at, the rabbit and wombat areas, the farms to avoid, and best places for setting a camp. After our gun choices, I practiced at least ten times this ritual—smell the barrel, click in golden bullets, slot in a magazine, open the bolt, cock the chamber, lift to shoulder, and sight test firing. I associate those times with positive energy and growth rather than with loss and grieving.

Now, without any bull, I recall feeling the bush spirit and the spirituality of Aboriginal Country, and I grieve for losing my naïve youth. There was the tired yarning by the fireside about who shot what and from how far. The beauty of twinkling stars through gum leaves. The sensuous sizzle of a rabbit being spit-roasted. The sticky goop of syrup and butter on hot damper. Luxuriously sleeping on fresh, shorn merino skin in the sheep shed. Dreaming with my Aboriginal ancestors about a bright future with a loving wife, sunshine, children, beach, and huzzahs. I take the happiness in the old hunting ritual to transform the trauma about my Aboriginal ancestors into a positive view of future Australia.

When the World ...

Sue Pincham

For a while after you died I saw you everywhere. Walking down the street, in a passing car, in the shop. The back of your head, your proud square shoulders. In profile, your nose, sharp and beaky.

Each time I started, drew a sharp breath. Once I tapped a man on the back in Woolworths, just to make sure.

'Jack,' I said. He looked alarmed, pulled away from me.

'Sorry,' I said, 'I thought you were somebody else.'

Other times I felt you rather than saw you.

A cool breeze on the back of my neck. The feeling of rain on my face when it wasn't raining. I didn't believe in such things before. I told Zoe about it, and I could tell she thought I had gone a bit mad, so I don't mention these things to others anymore.

Then there are those nights, when you came to the end of my bed – the bed that used to be our bed- and stood there. I tried to reach out to you but you vanished, just as suddenly as you had appeared.

Damn you for leaving me Jack.

Sometimes, when I couldn't sleep, I took a tranquiliser. I only did it rarely, at the very worst times, but they did help me get some rest. I was grateful for them in the very early days, but I knew they weren't for the long term. In any case, Dr Grace says she won't prescribe any more.

'You can't medicate grief,' she said.

She has been keeping a careful eye on me. She has been wonderful to me Jack, sitting with me time after time when all I could do was cry. She wants to send me to a grief counsellor, but I told her I feel more comfortable talking with her. It helps that she knew you too, and what we went through together in those last months.

Jack, when you died, I felt as if I had been turned inside out, put in a tumble drier and left to spin. The world didn't feel solid any more.

Friends and well meaning people tell me it is a matter of time. I wont feel your loss so deeply once a suitable amount of time passes. A lot of them say it might take a year, to get back on my feet so to speak.

They try to keep me busy, drop in for a cuppa, ring me frequently, take me for drives. I am grateful for their care and kindness.

But I just want you back Jack.

Buona Notte

Clara Rizzi

You look in the other direction when she calls your name. You hear the sound and turn to where she usually sits, no one there. No one there, your brow furrows, your ears point skyward, you feel footsteps penetrating through the pavement into your chest. In an instant you turn. Your black coat shimmers in the sunlight. Steady alert your brown eyes focus on her hands, her hands resting by her sides. Closer she draws and smooths your thick black coat.

Some days after a stroll in the park she combs your coat while you sit glancing sideways. You follow her down the white wooden stairs and sink into the sandpit. The sandpit under the pink camellia bush. She says, beve l'acqua, your brown eyes stare, you pant to cool. She repeats, Nero beve l'acqua. You lap the water and she says bravo. Some days she sits on the wooden stairs and gazes at the night sky, you slump beside her. The rhythmic words settle you, buona notte Nero. She disappears in the silent house.

A widow, strange word widow, strange dictionary meaning, 'a woman who lost her spouse by death and has not married again'. She didn't lose her husband, he died too soon. If he was lost there would be a chance to find him. She feels his presence in her dreams, his presence by the work of his hands, the folk songs he sang, the crosswords he left unfinished, the unchopped wood, the weddings and births he missed. Some say her late husband, she retorts late he was never late. He died too soon.

Step by step she climbs the stairs to the bedroom and is mesmerised by the winking stars, calls her husband's name into the vast silent still night. She aches with a yearning to stroke his warm hand. Remembers his last gasping breath, how they improvised the tango— his promise to dance.

Outside on the wooden decking Nero barks at a possum or neighbour's cat scurrying past. She wanders down the stairs slides the door, Nero *silenzio*, pats his soft furry head as he retreats into his kennel, *buona notte.*

Locked Away

Katherine Lothian

I thought I understood loss until this pandemic consumed the world and took my husband from me again.

Since Pete was diagnosed with Alzheimer's disease more than 12 years ago, I have mourned the loss of the man I fell in love with each and every day; my feelings of grief constantly regurgitated by this unrelenting disease.

Throughout that time, he has been at my side. Even as our lives descended into trauma and chaos and Pete moved into a care home, I continued to offer my daily dose of love and care, my emotions held at bay by his more immediate needs.

The COVID-19 virus brought with it a new and greater sense of loss than I could have imagined though. My husband was here but not here. Not only locked away in his own mind but now closeted in a care home with no access.

In 40 years we have rarely been apart but over the past year I've had to endure weeks and months at a time with no contact. The pain has been unbearable.

I logically understand that he no longer knows the people around him so he'd be fine with the amazing team of carers who have nurtured him for almost four years but I worry that there is something deep inside him that misses me, whether he was capable of recognising it or not.

Between March and July 2020, I was only allowed to peer in the window of the home on a couple of occasions, where I could see Pete hunched over in the lounge. Although they told me he was well, I was so desperate to put my arms around him and tell him that I missed him.

At times, we were told that we were no longer allowed to go onto the site of his home at all. By then, the country was in limbo with thousands of new cases and hundreds of deaths from COVID-19 each day.

Even after July, visits were sporadic at best. Residents were allowed one visitor, once a week, and those visits were held outside and I was only allowed to sit and talk to Pete from several metres away. Definitely no cuddles or kisses or singing allowed.

The last year has been heart-breaking, knowing Pete was still with me but without contact. Yet the moment I was allowed back into the home in

March 2021 and saw that sweet smile, feeling a connection so long absent, my heart soared once more. Seeing that sparkle in his eyes, that sense of lucidity, was magic, however disingenuous the impression was.

While I continue to grieve for everything that Alzheimer's and now COVID-19 have robbed me of, I am lucky to still have him, his tired smile reminding me that he is holding on to life.

Void Space

KL Morris

She tells me. Her voice shakes. Not like her at all.

'Dad's died,' she wobbles.

'When?' I ask automatically, even though we've known it would be soon.

'An hour ago,' squeaks my sisters voice, contorted through vocal chords that are betraying her.

I become conscious of the fact that I feel nothing.

I say, 'Do you want me to call anyone?'

'I already have,' she says.

My first thought is, '*Typical, she's already told my other sister and brother.*' I'm the youngest, I'm last even as an adult.

My next thought is, '*She's had to say those words three times.*' My heart breaks for her.

'I'll change my flight. I'll be there in the morning,' I tell her.

I think she says OK, but it could have just been a snuffle.

We say we love each other and hang up.

I become aware of my partner. He's awake beside me and he is close. I suppose from his side of the conversation: a three a.m. phone call, followed by a, 'When?' What else could it be?

'What's happened?' he says. I hear in his voice he already knows.

'Nothing,' I say. 'Go back to sleep.'

Why do I say this? I don't want to say the words?

'No, it's not nothing. What is it?'

I can't see him in the dark room. I'm on my back staring at the skinny strip of light that's broken through the blinds and stretched itself diagonally across the ceiling. He is on my side, his limbs around me like a boa constrictor.

'What's happened?' he pushes.

I draw breath.

'Dad died,' I say for the first time.

My partner lets out a sad noise. I don't know what its name is. He holds me tighter than I've ever been held.

He could squeeze the breath from me, lean all his weight on me. I feel no pain. I feel nothing.

I stare at the ceiling. I stare at that diagonal line of light and I register my lack of feelings. I examine the void space where emotions used to live. I peer at the emptiness with a vague curiosity. I try to make some sense of this. I can't.

'Really?' I think. *'Nothing?'*

Instead of grieving my father, I am numb. Incapable of processing a single emotion. Or is this grief? I don't know. I've never lost anyone I've loved before.

It would be days later, after my family had flown in from five directions to say goodbye. It would be after the little funeral when we could get up and depart, leaving Dad behind, when the first feel happened.

And it happened like a tsunami of ink rolling out of me. It poured from me like toxic rain, down my brothers shirt as he held me.

The Walking Dead

Linda Harding

I stumbled out of the cool shopping mall into the carpark, into the glare of a February day. Hands full of packages, I fumbled for my keys to the car. Not there. My broken self broke even more. The fog of grief I inhabited was thick; impenetrable. I was weighed down, confused and lost.

Two women with toddlers, babies in their arms, walked by me as I stood stunned beside my car with my heavy bags. 'I'm sorry,' I said, 'My four-year-old died two weeks ago and this is, I am, my first time out by myself, and I wonder, if you could hold, er, mind my packages while I, go get my keys, I left them, er, somewhere.' It came out in one long garbled sentence. Their faces registered every bit of shock and pity they felt. 'Sure,' they said, 'we'll wait.' Later I thought about the open-ended commitment they'd made, with their own children needing to be out of the hot sun and my emotional state obviously not conducive to thinking clearly and finding keys. But they did it, bless them, and I did find the keys fairly quickly at the bank where I'd left them.

When I got back one of the women said, 'I am so sorry you lost your child. Perhaps you need to go out only when there's someone with you, at least for a while. This is too soon.' It was, indeed, too soon. Part of me had known that, my inner parent was aware, but I had gone anyway. Grief had made me a zombie; I was the walking dead. I had died the day he drowned, and resurrection was not even on the horizon at that point. In truth, a month or so after this incident I died more deeply as the reality of his absence hit with greater force. He was no more.

Talking to those women I was struck by the strong urge I had to explain to everyone I met that he had gone … because this was who I was now. I was a woman who had lost her son. If you did not know that about me then you could not know me. Over 30 years later, I think that is probably still true, although the urge to tell has waned. We are our losses, as much as we are our achievements. I grieve therefore I am.

I wonder now when I venture out into the street how many out there are the walking dead. I pass by people that seem ok but maybe they're not. Perhaps their loved one has gone, and they are out too soon among the living; trying to do life when life has left them. I hope if I come across one of my fellow grieving zombies that I don't run. I want to react, as those compassionate women did, with patience and understanding and a tender willingness to help. The walking dead need so much love.

A Nameless Grief

David Terelinck

I walk the coastal dunes
we used to walk together.
She-oaks softly filter the breeze,
comb the last remaining light
from a late winter sky. Last night I dreamt
of you; held your hand as we strolled
this very path. We sat upon a fallen trunk.
I listened to your voice rise and fall
as you read from a slim volume
of Robert Frost. And when I woke,
to the absence of your words and breath,
it was as if you had died
all over again. And it's here that I come
to escape the silence that slips from the lips
of family and friends. They have stopped
dropping by with casseroles
and consolation. They don't mention
your name when they phone for fear
of upsetting me. I find myself not speaking
your name, find ways to spare their discomfort.
What gentle madness we've created
in politely striking you from our lexicon.
We talk of the weather, books we have read,
movies, the news of the world.
But there is such a strange emptiness
to every conversation. Our words are thin
and hurried; sanitised and scrubbed clean
of grief. Only the ocean doesn't mind endorsing
your name. I sign it onto the sand
with driftwood. The tide sweeps
in, swallows your name, washes it out to sea.
I call out your name and the wind
embraces it, and I think I hear you answer
in the cry of nesting terns.

Poem whose touch of river approaches

Shari Kocher

not water, but the artifice of oil on
brush stroked breast, spinning
grass lands whose knap hillsides
the velvet if seen from a window:
the gyrational force of a daisy's
deftness at work.

Yes, the eye of a flower *can* move the sun.

It doesn't have to ... be any less.
Haze of lilac on river bark, and all that rivers
in outline. I am almost just a moment.

I am not

accidentally walking into the line
of your looking, O busy whimsy: Behold.
Certain fathoms ripple backwards.

I shan't euphemise the grey in morning golds
as death is but one among the many
stout undertones that make me, frankly,
fearless in this modest self-appraisal.
Lively saffron & salmon speak the world

of a body at ease with mortality. So be it.

When I am done here, I shall wipe this brush
on cotton duck and take you with me, gladly.
A brown creek sounds over rocks like horsehair.

After the Fall

Diana Davison

It was the festive season but there was no jolly. Only hospital runs, the smell of disinfectant, busy nurses, doctor consultations and the start of the end. No remedies or recoveries or returning to the way things were. The worst week of my life, seeing my father slip away from me and being unable to fix him or bring him back. It was only after he died that I fully understood what palliative care meant. Did he realise when the stroke took up force on the battleground of his brain that he wouldn't be home for Christmas? It smothered and scourged him with his own blood to stake its claim. He tried to fight it, but by Boxing Day the enemy won. My memories only make me miss him more. The family seems incomplete without him. Five is an odd number. And now his energy is somewhere else instead of in my world.

Time has been patient with me, but my father's passing has not passed me by. I'm reminded of him on any corner at unassuming moments. Once, sitting in a cafe, I couldn't stop watching a grey-haired, elderly gentleman. He fashioned a white singlet visible under his pressed white cotton shirt, tucked into buckled up trousers. The same neat manner as my father used to dress, even during summer. I wondered if he too carried a handkerchief snug in his pocket. My father always did.

I hide a buried treasure in a top drawer of my dresser. A priceless folded white shirt patterned with faint pink and blue lines and a singlet. It is the shirt my father buttoned up for himself, then wore for the very last time. He ensured his appearance was smart in public. But for a game of bingo, it didn't work. He could not keep up with the numbers being called. I had to ring for an ambulance. Oblivious, it was to be our ultimate road trip together.

When driving nowhere, anywhere, I may see an aged man sauntering down the street, head shaded by a baseball cap or maybe just standing, reliant on his walking-stick. I'd have to do a double take … Dad? My mood quickly shifted into melancholy. He never left the house without donning his baseball cap during daylight hours. And venturing on walks made him happy. I loved our wanderings, united in company.

My father's wooden cane rests in my study. Sometimes I hold its handle, like I am holding on to his hand.

Unravelling

Carmel Summers

She pulls the first stitches from her needles
gently at first, watching cables slowly untwist.
She sees plains and purls arrange and rearrange
as she winds the length of creamy wool—eight-ply—
into a tight ball,
carefully tucking the end into its snug centre.

The sweater had been seamless, knitted in the round.
As she winds, the garment turns with a silent flop,
seeming not to become any less than it had been.

It had never been finished;
one in a series that had spanned their life together;
always cream, always wool, always arran.

She stares before her as her winding becomes fierce.
She appears aware of nothing else
as the ball grows larger
and the knitting is reduced to a band of ribbing
that could have been anything,
and finally, nothing.

The ball of wool slips from her finger
uncurling as it rolls across the floor.
She picks up the ball of wool.
Drops it.
Watches it unravel as it rolls across the floor.

14 January 2021

Grant Palmer

No feeding tube and you starved
Absent fluids your flesh withered
Drugs smothered your death
Polite terms for your reality
As you're promoted to glory

You failed the teachings of Jeremiah
Big Sis found the Lotto tickets
Evidence of your sin
My family whitewashing it away
Eulogising your sin free life

Your disgust of the gay
Your granddaughter's a lesbian
She is too scared to say
But she still loves you
Do you hate the gay?

Your body is ash
Now you are off to the stars
From where you originally came
Your last bet has now closed
So was Pascal right

Was your life worth the struggle?
Your beliefs based on an Iron Age book
For the sake of that wager
Yet I can still love despite all of that
Because I don't believe any of that crap

Birds of a Feather

Michael Cook

It has to be a minor chord. It's a cliché, but it's the only chord that fits.

My wife has just died and our two girls aren't yet ten. A minor chord is the one to play for Sammi—for all of us.

The Fender Telecaster is cold in my hands. I dial up the volume and fret a G-sharp minor chord. I stroke the strings with my thumb and let the sound reverberate around the room.

Sammi was our songbird—she always sang things better.

B-major and I grimace, hating the happy sound but knowing that it's part of this story. Happiness was our hearthstone for nearly twenty years, ever since Sammi and I met in a long-gone Y2K sushi bar during the jubilation of the Sydney Olympics.

When I run down C-sharp minor, I bend into the blues. This was the time of the realisation. This was me coming out of the bathroom, with toothpaste on my lip as I whinged about the constant barking of the dog next door. And then I saw Sammi—she was slumped over her book, her hair shrouding her face.

C-sharp minor and I'm wrenching it. This was me thinking that Sammi was having another one of her jokes—pretending that the book she was reading was the most boring thing in the world. I laughed and licked the toothpaste from my lip. When I plopped down onto the bed next to her, she rolled sideways and thumped head-first onto the floor.

A-sharp half-diminished, and I'm boiling it. Arpeggios whirl through the room. I lunged across the bed that night, 'Sam? What's going on?' She was heavy and limp, and it was a struggle to get her back onto the bed. Her eyes were still open, but there was nothing behind them. I started to panic.

As I hit the distortion, I know that the B string has snapped. The gap between G and E is a blank space, and that is perfectly right for this moment. Blank space.

The 000 phone call. The wait. The arrival of the ambulance. The girls all over me, 'Daddy, Daddy, what's wrong with Mummy?' Their voices harmonised and a detached part of me wondered if their mother's ability to sing has somehow been direct-loaded into these two little girls.

Distortion off, wah-wah on, riding C-sharp minor, just rolling the wheel of rhythm. This was the part when we waited in the hospital. This was when the mother-in-law arrived in her big Mercedes, came into the room and I saw her tremble like a leaf and all the distance between us fell away and we embraced.

I don't have a chord name for when the doctors came out and led us into a quiet, half-lit corner. There is no name for the feedback that pours from my Marshall, it is just colour, pain and all the time ahead without her.

Interstate Swimming

Siobhan Callan

WHEN I WAS five I fell into the Bright River. Victoria.
Splashingly, stepping too far away from my sisters
And brother—goggle-eyed, gulpingly—into the clear water.
I saw soundless silvery fish and current-blown ribbons
Of algae and weed, small streams of light falling down
From the river's surface, the water's force wallowing me
Up and tumble-turning me down. I held out my limbs
In wonder.
                    My mother, surf-swimmer and swimming teacher,
Stood on the bank. I saw her still body through the soft
Pressure of the liquid. Rescue me, I am drowning. But she
Didn't move. My father, English, who never learned
To swim, arrived at the river's edge and reached his arms
In and lifted me out. My mother wrapped my wet towel
Around herself and walked back to our borrowed house.
Now I am fifty-five, and my daughter's father died
Three years ago, and grief is not a bright river; it's a wide
Sea.

    On the news this week came the story of two men,
Missing on their way home in a wooden boat, drifting
From Coffin Bay, in a different state, when the engine failed.
That coast they say is wild: a surging pull of empty ocean
That could carry you down to the Antarctic. Yesterday,
Three days in, they found them: alive, floating, waiting
To be towed. From the boat I imagine them hearing

The cheering of wives, fathers, sons and daughters;
On the wharf, arms that have waited wrap them round
And warm them.
                                        Just now, I cold called my mother
Again. Two years since I heard anything. The phone
Rings and rings like an emergency without a response.
Time is a river she will not step in, and I am in it still,
Here in another state: Cootharaba, a shallow lake, flailing.

Stomping on Wildflowers

Virginia Tapscott

My sister and I had an unspoken, solemn bond of the kind that can only be forged in a mutual crisis. Alex helped me hide from our step grandfather in the night. I thought it was a game until he asked me to sit on his lap at the kitchen table one day when I was about four years old. He pulled down my knickers and his crusty old fingers hurt me until my Nan walked in and stopped him. When I told my older sister what had happened she plucked up the courage to tell our Mum. The abuse stopped, but the feelings of disgust and shame never left. We grew up feeling that we were defective.

A policeman called Darren walked into my mother's garden on a sunny winters afternoon and told her that her eldest daughter was dead. Mum fought for air and felt the Earth tilt beneath her. Then the words came spilling out. She found herself telling Darren the long held secret that had been lodged in her heart like a poisonous barb. After years of being sworn to silence, she was finally able to report the sexual violence that plagued her daughter.

My husband held me up while the waves of realisation buckled me at the knees. I went straight to her bedroom. Half looking for a sign from her to explain it all, and half looking for her. I wanted to touch the clothes that had last touched her skin. I wore her dark designer glasses around the house and smoked a cigarette from the packet we bought on our last night out together. I watched Friends repeats. I thought maybe if I could be her I could bring her back.

Family members pleaded with me to keep the assault of myself and my sister a secret. The expectation was that I would carry the pain so that everyone else could remain blissfully ignorant. They think I am the cause of this devastation but this has been a long time coming. The ripples built up to waves and who am I to hold back the tide.

People kept offering Mum a chair in the days following Alex's death but she kept insisting on sitting on the floor. I think she was trying to get a better grip on the earth as it swayed, an alien landscape without the child she birthed and held in her arms.

I remember the terror more than the sadness. The rising panic with each realisation that she wasn't coming back. I remember the resolve to start holding up our secrets like a cat at the back door with a dead bird in its mouth. I need everyone to look at the truth of what is happening in homes on every street, in every town in this country. To see what is happening. To see me.

Afterlife

Anne Morgan

Sing, dance and carouse for me,
but save your grief for the more deserving.
My life has been long enough; never straightforward,
but on balance, well worth the living.
Don't let me rest in peace.
I had time to rest when I was living.
When I am dead, put me to work
repaying my carbon debt with oxygen.

Marry me to a sapling, here on this high headland,
where I can pass messages through webs
of root and fungus to other tree folk.
Break out your pistils and stamens,
these rosellas will sip our nectar
and pollinate our blossoms.
The tiny pardalotes are back, foraging our leaves.
Let down your manna and feed them.
Lerps. Where are the lerps? Our crystalline honeydew?

Let my bare trunk be graffitied with the art of caterpillars.
Let my wood grow brittle beneath the stars,
comets and meteorites that have lent me their dust.
Let my fallen limbs provide high hollows for haunting owls
and dens for quolls and echidnas.
May children walk this headland
and watch, listen, smell, touch,
wonder.

The Gap

Lorne Johnson

I grip the endless clifftop fence with its rusted friendship
padlocks, bedraggled teddy bears and rattling Lifeline signs,

watch a pair of rainbows lifting from wolf-grey waters
lose their argument with incoming blankets of cold rain.

A southerly's breath rips apart a skywriter's love heart.
High cameras try to read what spins in our heads, what stirs

in our bones. Recently, a young tourist jumped this fence,
lost their footing for a selfie. Most days, lost loners linger

here, tracing the horizon line with shaky forefingers,
wondering how long it takes to swim to New Zealand.

There used to be a man they christened The Angel
of the Gap, who, for years, offered tea and sweet biscuits,

talked the fragile ones around ... I recall a wailing woman
who collapsed one night at the end of Shepherd Street,

near flats the colour of algae on a windswept tableland boulder,
and a vacant lot of barbed wire, indecipherable tags and scattered

rubble. This was before the great drifting from everything,
so I sat close to her as she wept, rocked. I offered my open palms,

my hollow words, until she calmed a little, thanked me,
said, *I've been kicked out of home. My teenage son has left*

me. God, I should be happy because I've been clean for a year.
I smiled, commended her, then a black SUV pulled up.

A teenage girl in a black Adidas hoodie got out, yelled, *Jesus,*
Mum. What the hell are you doing? Get in the car right now!

And the woman I'd sat with staggered away, didn't glance back.
The wind lashed wet pavement. I shivered, buttoned my coat,

wandered home past overflowing bins, ruptured downpipes,
fractured terraces. Hidden hounds howled: ambulances wailed

sympathetically. Outside Carriageworks, I stared up at two words
pulsing in red neon: REMEMBER ME. A distant moaning

from train stabling yards, or our defeated, retreating Milky Way.
A humming cyclist, cradling a bunch of white lilies, slipped

out of the street's bleeding dark, her silver headlight blinding.
From a warm, purring machine in her jacket pocket,

a trail of silver bubbles like a fresh, streaming universe.

Kissing the hand of your Enemy

Peter J Wells

Is any space
not contested
by culture, language, and history?

By sexual identity?
By stories of a socio-economic bent?
By spit-balling and political point scoring?

The Good Friday agreement
was a mathematical equation
claiming

two separate nations
equals
one place

and down came the gun towers
and the barbed wire was plucked
like a hair from food

and compromise
was embedded in a constitution
like a delicate skin

on cooling custard
and both nations
let it sit

till longer begat longer
and they tried to learn
this new life

in the face
of their dear, dear ghosts
and their ruined kneecaps

all the time knowing
reconciliation, like love,
is impossible.

stages

Ashleigh Mounser

I. We could keep burning the skin around it forever and ever. How many pounds of flesh for a life? Another doctor in another white room with another chart might say something different, have they tried looking at it on the side, what would happen if you never let go, if you never gave up then maybe

II. I hold myself like a fist, tensed for impact. I'm furious in the shower, glowering on the bus. Everyone who turns out not to be you is my enemy, a deep chasm of disappointment separates me from everyone else. I hate the postman, I hate the woman buying low sodium teriyaki sauce and somehow, I still have enough left to hate my friends. I remember that feeling years ago at the red light, your foot on the brake, when you saw the car coming behind us in the rear-view mirror, when you squeezed my hand and told me to brace myself for what couldn't be stopped

III. If I'd had another year, if I'd known sooner what I know now, if I hadn't been young and thought that time was an infinite resource, if I hadn't been so

IV. I held his hand, didn't say anything cruel like I wanted, anything like *please don't leave me.* Anything selfish like *what about me here alone*, not knowing how to poach an egg, if it's righty-tighty, lefty-loosey, can you tell which way is north by looking at how the sun falls? You are peaceful at the end, like I wanted, like I was afraid you would be. You are ready to leave me behind. I blink and the heat has left your hand, your heart. If your eyes are still warm, I can't see them so it doesn't matter. I don't buy into false gods or holy spirits. There is no need to watch the weatherman guess, I go outside and discover that it is not raining. These are the facts. No rain, no you now that the coroner has come with his white sheet and his eyes sombre on the rug, no howling into the wind for me

V. Over a glass of wine, my aunt asks me if I'm over it, and I drink instead of saying something which will make everyone uncomfortable. I find myself doing that a lot. I drink instead of saying that I will never get over it, that I never want to, that I carry it with me, some days I wake up and remember all over again in a rush, a train barrelling towards me, the wheels chug *gone-gone-gone*. That gasp in the morning, that sob over risotto at night is the only thing I have left of you. On Friday, for the first time I woke up and felt something new, something like a version of myself returning to my body, clawing back in to where it thinks it belongs, trying to fit around the loss, the space reserved for your absence.

Animal Rescue

Anne Zito

On the day you leave the boarding house, you pack up your things without a word. No text, no note, no money. A cat pushes open our door and curls up on the bedspread. Night after night the cat's eyes shimmer; it plants its head in the small of my back, purrs and I'm rocked to sleep. One morning, the sun slides under the door and the cat is no longer mine.

Cold rain

on the sign

No vacancy

Coming Back as a Bird

Rod Usher

I'd always said Spring's harbinger,
a pilot to embarrass the Red Baron,
the holy hero of *The Happy Prince.*

I got older, started leaning Cormorant,
majority here on our wide river,
outvoting even the ducks.
Above and under it they doubly fly,
hang themselves out in the sun to dry.
But … silent, those black feathers
oiled as Elvis's hair?
And certain people would declare:
'I always knew he'd end in rant.'

Age making us ever more comical,
now I'm putting myself down
for the one some call the avian clown.
Fast as a Penguin under water,
also a brilliant air-swimmer,
triangular red beak like no other,
plus black, white, yellow,
a burrower rather than nester.
God must have been tipsy
when He designed such a jester,
Chaplin in technicolour.

No, leave the Eagle to mere dominion,
Crow to his continual complaining,
Owl to the acquired taste of fieldmice,
Seagull to scream and scavenge,
Sparrow to crumbs of junk food.
It's the circus next life:
Puffin!

Skin Hunger

Emma Grey

My husband never passed me a glass of champagne without his fingers brushing mine.

He'd touch the small of my back with every, 'Have you met my wife?'

He'd pull me into his arms as we passed in the hallway at home ... less ships in the night, more stolen kisses at bookshelves.

He'd kiss my forehead, leaving for work after an interrupted night with the baby, or when I was mid-scene in my writing and couldn't lose my train of thought.

His hand found mine on the cobbled streets of Paris and Florence and London, pulling me away from traffic and crowds and into bookshops and cafes.

His thumb would stroke my knee in movies. Our legs would touch under tables, our arms entwined on armrests, fingers threaded through each other's.

I'd feel his hands on my hips, gently shifting me aside so he could reach a kitchen drawer, or pass something over my head.

He'd press his hand to my forehead when I was sick and stroke my arm when I was upset and he was worried.

He'd tuck the tag of my shirt into the collar at my neck and brush the inside of my wrist fastening a bracelet. He'd sweep my hair aside and unclasp a necklace or undo a button or loosen a zip.

He'd thread his fingers through my hair and draw my lips to his and drag his fingertips down my spine because he loved the way my back would arch at his touch.

I'd feel the weight of his arm across my body as he slept. Trace the hairs and the freckles on his skin. Feel the stubble on his chin as it brushed my face. When he was freshly shaven, I'd place my cheek to his, inhaling his aftershave, the last bottle of which I still have because the lingering scent lets me close my eyes and pretend...

My head would rest on his shoulder, standing jet-lagged in arrivals halls. His arms would wrap around me in 'hello' and 'goodbye' and in 'everything will be okay'.

But it was not.

And it's his incidental touch I miss the most. Touch that shows instead of tells. Touch between soulmates—the absence of which gives you 'skin hunger', and not for just anyone. *Him.*

Psychologists say some couples touch up to 180 times in an hour. Five years has robbed me of 43,800 hours and millions of gentle interactions that felt like home.

We crave it, that contact. The comfort. The tenderness. The sense that we're facing this world together. We crave it from the day we are born, when we're dependent on it. When we fall and graze our knees. Or our hearts.

We crave it as forty-something widows who had it, facing fifty years without it.

Surviving Identity Grief Through Resilience

Mark Lock

from a white skin First Nations Ngiyampaa Australian

'Wish you were like the real blacks,' whip-cracks Nan,
Gutted I spluttered, 'I'll go for a full body black tattoo then!'
'Yeah,' demeans the Elder 'like dem territory guys',
Her brown eyes spear my blue eyes,
My spirit bleeds.

'Those blacks have the *reallll* culture,' romanticises she,
Blood-up in my face. 'Should I change my DNA?' in me,
'Yeah,' jabs older MDMA brother. 'Take a shot of Dreamtime!'
His black skin-from quarter kin-is more valued than mine,
My soul splits.

One side is where fair people advance Australia,
The other side is for stolen Dreaming regalia,
'You are an *f*-en mistake!' slurs drunken mother,
A product of Nan's choice of a white convict lover,
My toxic anti-matter mix.

Black lives matter and white skins shatter,
Aboriginal cultural purity and colonial culture poison,
Black power and white disempower,
Koori or gubba questions me a twisted rhyme,
Where my self is a thorny Songline.

'Behave like a real man!' glares Uncle Abuser,
Heat in my cheeks to him 'how many rape kids have you, user!?'
Slap! Beer bottle shatter brings silence,
I watch blood relatives cringe in shamed conscience,
Initiating my bashed identity.

Years later 'Behave like a gentleman' opines the awarded Oxford professor,
With fiery retort to him 'like your ancestors to mine? *Sir*',
Tap! His keyboard cleaves me. 'I'll replace you with another Man Friday',
It's the usual privileged violence *once a day*,
Which forces me into bitter compliance.

Buried is the grieving for my contorted spirit-soul-self-identity,
For I'm not authentic enough for anyone's reality,
Not traditional, not a real black, not ceremonial, not speaking language, just NO(T)!
The thorns of knots prick bleed me with sounds of crack-lash-bash-shot-slap-tap-silence
But I fight back-YES!-exorcising grief with resilience.

Tear-Soaked Shirts

Tom Eskdale

For the longest while I was numb.

The tears wouldn't come. My memories were just detached images of her. A blurry face cloaked with dirty blonde hair saying things.

In the kitchen, 'It's cold today, take your jumper.'

At the school gates, 'Love you, darling.'

At my bedroom door, 'Goodnight, don't get out of bed.'

In my dreams she was distant and unreachable. I dreamt of empty liquor bottles and a shuddering body in the dark; her hand waving through the elevator doors before they closed, and the dented boot of her white Toyota Camry as she sped away. When I woke, I'd never know if I had been crying or not.

I'll keep busy, I thought. I'll play soccer and surf and do my homework twice to distract me. I saw my sister and dad crying and I wanted to cry with them; but I couldn't. The tears wouldn't come. Am I a sociopath? I thought. Did I even love my Mum? Is something wrong with me?

My family were worried about me.

'This is how a lot of kids deal with grief,' said our doctor.

Me, dad and my sister started going to a suicide bereavement support group once a month. I enjoyed these nights. We took the long drive down south and got drive-through Maccas on the way. It was nice to spend time together away from school and work. At the group I never said anything. I just sat and listened. One elderly woman spoke about her husband who left a goodbye note saying sorry. She cried and accepted tissues and then poked fun at herself for being an emotional old lady. I was munching on a shortbread bikky at the half time break when she came up to me. She told me how brave I was. I really liked that lady, but I felt a pang of guilt looking into her bloodshot eyes, thinking about the horror they had seen.

For the longest while I was numb. I felt heartless. Empty.

I was looking through my bookshelf one night and picked up a book I hadn't read in a while. I opened the cover and on the inside was her trademark overly large handwriting.

To my dearest Andy, because u luv reading.

It hit me hard. My heart jumped up six gears, my face clenched and the tears jumped out hot and furiously. A panic. Every memory of her came at once. The glint in her hazel eyes, her boisterous laugh, her desperate weeping and her warm body.

I realised she was never coming back, and my world felt smaller than ever as I gasped for breath, drowning, with the room swirling and the bedroom walls closing in on me. The door swung open and my Dad and sister were there beside me. We cried and cried, holding each other tight until our shirts were soaked and there were no tears left.

Ruby-Throated Hummingbird

Kerry Greer

Ruby-Throated

Leaning in, hummingbird over nectar,
Wings as heartbeats when you
So casually kissed me,
As if it was some
Everyday thing.

Hummingbird

I made you wings of paper
Shaped like aeroplanes,
Light as ashes.
I blew them up to you
Every time I blew a kiss.

With the wings I gave you
My grief moulded back
Into love, not heavy as sacred
Pillars of Herod's temple,
Destroyed where they stood.

They said I couldn't send
You love, that you weren't there
To receive it, so what I sent was still
Grief, a monolith like the Western
Stone of the Wailing Wall.

I said, Have you ever felt the breeze,
diaphanous,
Dry your tears, as you gazed upon the sea?
Do you not think that is him kissing me
With his wings
In every beautiful thing I see?

Sail

Willo Drummond

In an instant you are a sail
loosed, flapping. Sprayed

with a sea of tiny blades—
a vast, over-sensate skin. Your silent

voice, a gaping mouth, calls
from a crack in the world: *desolate*

wind, sweep my knowledge
into oblivion, drop me back

in the well; all that sounds is the clink of flailing
shackles against the mast.

Experience says, in time,
the canvas will snap

taut. Right now
this sheet is the shape of living.

The ladder's blown
the world's all wailing wind.

Notes

Terminus

Bette Martin

The mother holds the phone against her ear. She detects a faint sob, then another, louder.

Her stomach churns, eyes fill then overflow.

'Mum,' a voice wails.

'I'll be right there.' The mother rushes to the garage, keys in hand.

The front door stands ajar, the mother rushes in to find her daughter cowering on the couch. She enfolds her sobbing daughter in a gentle embrace.

'It may not be too late.' The daughter lifts her head, contradiction in her eyes.

They're entering the Hospital Casualty Room. Her daughter steps gently, slowly. Several pairs of eyes sweep over them then away. Her daughter chooses a seat in a shadowy corner, avoiding the golden patches of sunshine pouring through the skylights. She sits, eyes down, wrapped in a grey cloak of her own misery trying to merge into the afternoon shadows.

It's their turn. Her daughter dictates as the nurse fills in the required details. Name, age, address.

'How far along?' Tears sprout again.

'Eleven weeks I think or maybe twelve. No, no eleven weeks, twelve was last time … or maybe the time before.'

'Go through the security door and into the examination room first right.' The heavy glass doors hiss open, her daughter passes through, more waiting. The mother sits outside on a cold plastic chair in silence. She waits, and waits. She wonders what would happen if she gave in, just let go. Opened her mouth wide and allowed the screams swirling round and round in her brain to escape. Would they spiral like black smoke around and upwards, fill the air with pain, rage?

Not fair! Not fair!

The mother knows she needs to stay calm. She stiffens her posture, clamps her teeth together as the doctor approaches to communicate with her eyes, words which need not be spoken. A nurse hovers in the doorway, avoids eye contact. She moves off and the mother and daughter trail along behind. Through doorways, around corners, past curtain enclosed rectangles where other people deal with their own particular pain.

They're ushered into a small room. The mother settles her daughter down in the bed. Weak daylight filters through tree branches outside the one window high up in the wall. Her daughter closes her eyes, overcome with physical and mental pain. The mother holds her daughter's hand as she lies restless in the bed. Soft moans echo in the room as the young woman writhes. Stomach muscles pulse-squeeze-ease, as they expel her hopes and dreams. The afternoon is waning, daylight ebbs away.

The window rattles in its frame as the door silently swings open. Nurse pierces soft flesh to insert a morphine drip. Twenty minutes later her daughter's body relaxes, she lies still, head rests on the damp pillow, eyes close as she drifts along the river of forgetfulness. The mother hears muffled voices from the next room, then the soft cry of a newborn fills the air.

The daughter sleeps. The mother slumps in her chair and weeps.

Brother Ocean

Mykaela Saunders

My brother has become the ocean -
From where we all came, he went and returned,
his sadness too big for his own immense heart within a body
that carried the wounds of centuries through ancient black blood
from saltwater people swimming with strength through his veins.
The ocean: the only body big enough to contain him.
He made it his deathbed, his heaven, his home.

The ocean has become my grief -
I sit on our beach for hours at a time and
grief cracks my heart and pours into the sea.
Waves crash with violence and water boils over the sand to meet me,
then recedes, melting back gently in its ebb.
I adjust my weeping in accordance with its flow
to enter these rhythms of our new relationship with respect.

My grief is oceanic -
Held beneath the surface of living by death, I drown
under the weight of my loss every day. Roughed and tumbled
and strangled in its vortex, scoured into purity by salt and sand.
In moments of release I break the surface, gasping, and draw breath
just in time to be held down again. When I emerge
the ocean leaks from my eyes; I drip my lament wherever I go.

The ocean has become my brother -
Journeying his ashes across glass waves,
we return him to the ocean—his ossuary—
in a ceremony of release for us left behind to heal.
Under the water, I send him off in song;
air escapes my throat and returns to the sky.
The ocean welcomes my tears back home.

My brother has become my ancestor -
I fill a bottle with seawater to take home with me.
Beside my bed, my brother's spirit holds me safe
as I sleep and my grief seeps from my body to talk to him.
He listens to my loss, holds my pain gently,
and feeds our stories back to my sleeping spirit.
In my dream we are still swimming and laughing together.

The Three Sisters

Melitta St Just

We climbed to the top of the Mountain. We did it for our Joseph, for us. It's his birthday; he would have been 35 had he not died by his own hand. We dragged ourselves to the top, out onto the outcrop. It was like no other climb we had ever done, we are older now our bodies less conditioned, our hearts heavy with loss. We pressed our aching, battered bodies against the cold granite, the space was barely wide enough to accommodate the three of us. Somehow we managed to melt and mould our bodies onto the ledge. We reached out one at a time, three times each, taking it in turns. Nine. We had to get all nine of the rocks out there placed one atop the other. Though small, the rocks were heavy. They are people. Each is a person. After the last rock was placed, we slid back one at a time. We longed for it to be over, yet enjoyed having had this moment of closeness. We did it. The cairn is on the ledge. Our cairn. Our family. Made by the three sisters.

Mine is just dentistry, thus I can pray for my oldest friend

James Walton

I lack the faith of doorknobs or roads
the steadfast purity in purpose
an exhibit of solid testimony
between before during now and after
how hands or rain or dust cannot shake
the utility of being so

no minor inconvenience for direction
no reason to look beyond or under
but then doubt is a quiet virtue
applied as it is to wax over an incisor
to blunt a broken molar at the tongue
to pace the slow words

thus I can pray for my oldest friend
while the aloof surgeon intercedes
to halt the spread of decades
this wily thing remorselessly pacing
our born shadow gift and terror
mine is just dentistry

a contiguous shallow emergency
for the same day as your anaesthesia
maybe I can ask for something else, gas?
journey together to a dreamy theism
take hold of our resiling years
palm to brass handle, knee to bitumen

Ulysses

Suzi Mezei

I press an open palm to my belly. Something moves deep inside. There's a soundless, sharp upheaval; the tearing away of a promise.

The medics smear me in gel, hold a Doppler over a tiny rise that refuses to believe I'm not pregnant. But the cramps have already started. The scanner glides over the vacancy inside me. No heartbeat; just watery silence.

What have I done? What haven't I done? I will always wonder. Guilt crushes me.

A tide shifts. It draws away. I am left behind.

After I am cleansed of failure, surgically scratched clean, woken from an anaesthetic torpor, they tell us to wait 'til we try again.

The healing's slow.

We find the image of him, our boy, a cluster of white interconnected dots, a galaxy of miniscule constellations against a backdrop of black gloss. My husband seals the print in an envelope, tucks it away in a small box of irreplaceables.

We make new plans. Although I'm an atheist, I ask my mother to pray.

But it happens again; and again. Plans and prayers end in a gush of loss. I return from hospital, a plastic band still attached to my wrist. I'm stuck on replay, re-visiting the same moment. I crumple like the pile of clothing discarded on the bathroom floor. I hide in the shower steam, wash the stickiness from my body and attempt to dilute my grief.

I stare into a grey godless sky.

They say it's natural, we're born with it; the ability to make new people, to fill our homes with the sounds and machinations and raw, joyous potential of small human beings.

But it's not.

They say it's a gift.

But some will never receive it and others will spend years searching empty rooms believing they've misplaced it.

My daughter parks her Jeep at the edge of the rose garden. We grew it to remember the children we lost, those tiny promises that weren't kept.

Nature shows us that every bud will not bloom. But when they do, they colour the world.

I remember the Christmas Eve before she was born. The house was ripe with the scent of honeysuckle. I placed my husband's hand on my belly. Inside, there was a flutter of butterfly wings; Blue Ulysses, Monarchs, Yellow Admirals. Inside, someone new waited.

Butterfly wings. We held them tight. We were lifted.

The Final Meal for a Gentle Man

Dee Murdoch

As a reformed pipe smoker, Dad loved food. The morning ritual of gluten-free cereal, milk, yoghurt, two cups of black tea with honey, a banana and to finish off a perfectly peeled orange. All consumed at the table, never on his lap, with linen serviette and silver serviette ring, sideplates and the correct assortment of cutlery.

The time after breakfast he spent with a book or meticulously sorting through a finite collection of current bills and bank accounts, or checking over the documentation relating to the arrangements for the donation of his body to the university. All of these were stored in an arch lever folder, together with a bundle of stamped, addressed and sealed envelopes that were to be posted upon his death—the opening line of the letter stating, 'If you are reading this then I am dead'.

At 93 he was quick witted, rational and astute. It was his body that was letting him down. A bullet in his shoulder, deafness, and an injured leg—the result of his war experiences as a paratrooper, were overshadowed by his heart which simply couldn't keep up with the pace of life that he wanted to live.

His determination for laughter, love and longevity were demonstrated by his waiting for me to return from a year long posting with Red Cross to Kenya. Whilst we had said our goodbyes before I left, he held out for my home coming. My first week back in Australia was a special time together sharing stories, fish and chips, long drives and quiet moments.

The phone call is one that no one wants to receive.

'Dearest Bugs, I have just phoned the ambulance. Could you please meet me at the hospital?'

He made his final decline with dignity and love. His resolve showing through to the last hours as he insisted on getting up to shower and most importantly, to go to the toilet. Whilst his appetite faded, he always insured the hospital menu card was completed with every possible option ticked—all of course labelled gluten-free.

The final morning was a time for family as we gathered around his bed and chatted of life, love, sadness, times past and yet to come.

Lunch arrived. Soup, a simple salad, fruit and custard. Propped up in bed with an arrangement of pillows he sipped the soup, passed on the salad, though eyeing the fruit and custard he declared he would enjoy it.

With assistance from my sister he sampled the dessert, commenting that he hoped the custard was gluten-free.

Lying back, he smiled at us, closed his eyes and took his final breath.

How could I grieve his death? He had lived a full life and died with the dignity that a gentleman desires. There was no funeral or cremation but weeks later we gathered together to celebrate his life and not to mourn it.

Dorothy

Mark Mahemoff

Dorothy was an ex-nun who lived on our street.
She seemed content to be the local sticky beak.

We could hear her at night, alone in her bedroom,
in heated conversation with an enigmatic past.

Then one day, inexplicably, her house became silent.
No one was eager to ask too many questions.

Her life confronted us with the mess of existence,
the untidiness most of us try to efface.

Our street was the place where Dorothy once lived.
Dorothy's death now lives here in in its place

My Father's Hands

Asha Rajan

In memory, my father's hands are large
sturdy fingers, columns that hold the Parthenon
pillars that secure the world on the turtle's back
that hold me as I swing between him and my mother

Palms span wide, encompass mine
welcome his new wife to a new country, cradle his children
hold together a family, welcome new migrants
embrace everyone as if they're family

In memory, his hands are warm and safe,
a harbour, a guide, a beacon

They are surety

His hands tell stories;
of squirrels caught and tamed
placards held and fists raised
careers relished then signed away

They hold his love and patience
anger too

In memory, my father's hands are brown like mine
with large pores and deep creases at the knuckles
nails bitten short nubs that punctuate fingers.

His palms, beach sand, plump
ridged with warm umber lines that mark fate,
life,
fortune

His wedding ring
my mother's initial on its face
rests on my index finger

Hands that spanned continents, embraced lives
were only slightly larger than my own

All giants of memory shrink

The Universal Language of Grief

Kathryn Gardner

Once upon a time, I believed that the grieving process began when a loved one passes away. To me, this seemed logical as I believed that grief was the result of death. Little did I know that my understanding would change completely when my daughter was diagnosed with a terminal degenerative disease!

Although our daughter was still very much alive, we grieved for her and for everything that she would never get to experience. She would never walk or run, she would never know the fun of going to kindergarten or school, she would never get to make friends, eat chocolate, fall in love, have a career or have a family of her own. As a parent, perhaps the hardest part of all was that she would miss out on going through life with her beloved sister, and that her sister, myself and my husband would forever feel the void of living without her.

My new found understanding of grief and the many layers of the grieving process got me thinking about how universal this experience was for everyone all around the world. At some stage throughout life, everyone will be touched by grief regardless of their gender, race, culture, religion or any other differentiating factors. Some people will grieve for lost loved ones or friends. Some will be touched by tragedy or health issues that will forever impact their physical ability, leaving them to grieve for the full and healthy life that they will no longer have. Infertile couples and individuals may grieve for biological children that they will never have.

Despite the commonality of grief, it is often a taboo subject which makes people feel uncomfortable to discuss openly. So many people don't know what to say to someone grieving so they say nothing at all. Some will unintentionally say the wrong thing even though they had the best of intentions. How can we know the right thing to say when different people grieve in so many different ways? What might be the right thing to say to one person may be the wrong thing to say to another.

My personal journey with grief has evolved. What I needed in the early days following my daughter's death is different to what I need now. For such a long time I struggled to contain my emotions… anytime someone mentioned my daughter or anything that triggered thoughts about losing her, I was an absolute mess. I remember having mixed feelings… I wished that people wouldn't mention her as I didn't want them to see me cry; yet I also felt grateful that they were brave enough to speak to me and offer their love and support. Years later, I have become more resilient and can talk about my daughter without bursting into tears. In fact, I appreciate when people remember her.

Grief is universal and multi-faceted with no perfect solution to support the bereaved yet reaching out and making an effort means so much!

The Birthday Party

Sara Green

You in petticoats, all sugared-almond pink, and shiny shoes;
Tight pigtails zagged across your head,
And me in shorts, jelly-smudged, bare-toed and dusty.

Black maids in crisp white aprons,
Children hanging from their hems like paw-paws,
While our mothers sipped champagne.

You hid behind your mother's skirts:
It wasn't fear of alligators lurking in the lake beside our garden,
Nor coral snakes in cane fields, never still with rustling,
Nor the Donkey Man, his band of threadbare donkeys
Swarmed by kids for rides that pinched our thighs and bruised our bottoms.

Years later, you told me you were mortified.
Years later, when I nursed you: the cancer spread before your cough betrayed it.
Your life spilled from every closet then; each surface bore a story.
Never so ordered in life as you were in dying.
All clutter culled, you leave me with this date to mourn you.

Your mother dressed you like a doll, puff sleeves and patent leather,
While we young ruffians built sandcastles, threw water-filled balloons.
It never left you, this agitating grain of childhood,
This grain, which grew into a pearl inside my palm.

When the box tree is no longer

Yvonne Deering

For Sylvia

Year after year
the woodswallows return
to summer in the box tree
by the river

hearing their voices high I know they have arrived
white flecks of freelife flittering skimming skipping
across the sky

Year after year
my summer upward gazing dizzies me
until along a limb I see
the swallows settle

close to the nesting hollow
white breast beside white breast
dark-hooded huddle

Year after year
I hear the caterwaul
of chainsaw laying claim
of treemaul treefall

see rising side by side
more riverfront dwellings
with water views

Year after year
I wonder
where the woodswallows will summer
when the box tree is no longer

April 1940 The Soldier

Patricia O'Shea

April 1940

Eric reboarded the train; the same compartment with the stale fug of Woodbines and the sweat of fellow recruits.

This time it was silent and empty. The camaraderie and anticipation of adventure and danger abandoned on Chatham platform. He looked at the crumpled telegram still in his hand and checked his pocket for the return ticket and seventy-two hour leave pass. With his kitbag as a pillow he lay on the seat, his greatcoat a blanket against the void of the overnight return.

He knelt in the front room, curtains drawn against the weak April sunlight. Knots of the pegged rug—slivers of rags from long worn-out clothing—pressing through the rough material of his new uniform. His head bowed in tear-wet hands, helping to stifle the insidious sweetness of decaying lilies and acrid disinfectant, carrying something far more primal in its wake. It would never leave him, never; this smell of poverty and death. And the chill of his mother two days dead in the cheap, sad coffin.

'I'm having that, he'll not want it. He'll not be back here.'

Greedy, greedy aunts. The older and the younger, the fat and the thin, flapping wings over the meagre spoils in the back room.

He put his hands over his ears. He could die of loneliness.

The front door opening and the warmth of a hand on his shoulder.

'Come with me lad. We'll come back later and sit with her tonight.' Mrs Rutter, childless, widow, defender, rescuer, and seventy if she was a day, opened the door to the back room. She lunged towards the sisters with her walking stick.

'You should be ashamed of yourselves. I heard you from two doors down!'

Harriet opened her mouth. Rose visibly flinched. The stick loomed above them.

A hiatus.

He thought she would strike them, cracking their brittle skulls like hard boiled eggs.

'Call yourselves Christians—his mother's dead in the next room and you haven't got the decency to wait 'til she's in her grave!'

She led him through the kitchen and out to the back yard.

'Your home's with me now, lad. I've made up the spare room.'

An old rusty pram stacked to the brim was parked under the open window.

'I've got a wheelbarrow if you want the blasted bricks as well!'

It was the only time he would hear her swear.

'I hope she comes back to haunt you!'

Safe in her own house, she handed him a thin gold wedding band.

'She wanted you to have this.'

And a simple wooden clock.

'It was all I could save.'

He took it in both hands, the gentle vibrations of a heartbeat.

'I'll keep it on the mantelpiece and I'll wind it every night, until you come back.'

Endurance

Erin A. Sayers

When the news came through, somewhere deep in my gut, I already knew. Unlike his sister and parents, all graced with a humble 'I love you', I'd had the sign off.

'I can't find anyone to love me.' But I loved you.

'I feel like shit. Do you ever feel like this?' All the time. But we'd talked about it before. So many times. It was just a rehash of the same conversation we'd had a thousand times before.

Three days later, my 'are you ok' never reached him.

Being part of a large family, it fell to a small few of us to phone-tree the news around. Within minutes, the story was changing, warping, turning a choice into an accident.

Depression is a disease, one I knew with haunting familiarity. Passing all that pain off as an accident is humiliating to all those who carry it. Dying from depression is just as serious as any other disease.

COVID caused everything to slow to a trickle. We were in lockdown less than two weeks after and his body was still stuck in Europe. I didn't see my family for months. No one was talking. Every death-positive neuron in my brain was trying to find a way to process everything, wanting to help but powerless to act. My own depression swallowed me; a constant embrace around my chest.

The first time I met up with the planning committee, a small family group born from memorial preparations, I didn't cope. Ignorant words were said by some; my bipolar causing my own breakdown. I was angry, stuck in a rotating door of emotions. I'm now scared of those people.

The new year comes around. I ask if the memorial is going to happen on the anniversary. Someone in the family contacts me, telling me to mind my own business. He wasn't my brother, just my cousin. My grief isn't important and keeping my thoughts to myself is the 'right thing' for the family. The depression I'd managed is back, howling in my ears. Two weeks of my life disappear into darkness. I'm broken all over again.

The memorial goes ahead, the day graced with torrential rains and storm warnings. Fitting. I say my piece, standing in front of the assembled. I planned ahead, walking the line between sincere and cautious. I know it's not enough but it's a start. I'm numb, empty of feeling and thought. More time passes. Now I won't see anyone till Christmas. The cycle repeats.

I realised a few things. To me, he was more important that the rest combined. Our relationship was special, too good for this world. He saw me and I him. They can't take that from us. True, time changes everyone. But no matter how the family whines and bickers, he made me strong. I got my first tattoo, just for us. I wrote about him, using my words to process and immortalise.

He taught me endurance. And I will endure.

Brokeheart Blues

Jo Lyons

I'm at the post office
sending you a gift
wrapped in black
paper tied with
white ribbon
your name
in cursive.

The lady gives me
a hard time
is it going
somewhere
          far away
                    overseas
                              intergalactic

I don't know

Each time
I look down
the present
unravels
laying bare a box
of chalk pastels
in broken blues
          cobalt
                    cerulean
                              ultramarine

crumbling
to dust

On waking
I set up the studio
get out my blue
inks and pastels
start a drawing

my first in years.

Spring 2020

Beth Clapton

I thought that you would wait
        with simple decorum
just beyond the frame until
        your moment came
with the lowering of the blinds.

But you
                mistimed
your entry - like an understudy
over-eager with her lines. You barged in,
                and found me unready.

Through Spring you whispered -
        he will not see these blossoms fall, nor taste
        the apples born of the labour of those bees
I cannot recall – did those trees bear fruit at all?

One morning I climbed the long hill to the village
you chose that moment to remind me
        how his strong hand at my back, once gave the power
        my young legs lacked.
                The warm pressure rests there still.

At dinner you would grip my stomach
        in your icy fist.
        insist he could not taste
his favourite dish,
                that all my labour lay in waste.

On his last night I took the book from beside his bed
and found you
            interleaved
in the unread pages - light fingered as a mirror
        stealing yesterday's reflection.
        I shook you loose
and made you wait as I offered him
        this last protection – I told him
how the story ends.

Grieving Before She's Gone

J. F. Bolton

There was a kind of intense boredom to it. Everything moved so slowly. He was sitting close to her bed, occasionally reading from a book he'd brought. Sometimes he would read to her, and other times he would simply stare out the fifth floor window into a staff parking area and grieve for a person who hadn't yet gone.

He hated it. He didn't want to spend time with her in this way. He wished these wouldn't be his last memories of her. But it wasn't up to him anymore; these were the only memories left, and he wanted those memories. Oh, God, did he want them! He clutched desperately at every slow and exhausting second he could get with her. Time was slipping uncaringly between his fingers like a handful of water in the desert.

Others in the family still had hope. His father and sister thought she'd pull through. They thought that miracles happened. People survived cancer all the time, and it could happen here, too. He knew better. He had knowledge and training. He lived in the medical world. The cancer was too large. It pushed on too many important places.

It all seemed so unfair. She had dogs at home that hadn't seen her in weeks, small, gentle creatures that longed for her and didn't understand where she'd went. There was a one-year-old grandson who would never know her at all. All the boundless love for the people and animals in her life was about to go with her, inch by inch, second by agonising second. It didn't matter. None of it mattered.

It was just. So. Unbelievably. Cruel.

And he was tired. He'd been there many hours and he would stay for even longer. Today was special. The surgeon was willing to try something, a last minute effort. It was a Hail Mary, a last desperate pass in the game, a sacrificial light cavalry charge into artillery fire.

It was doomed. He knew this. The surgeon had explained that it would be painful, life-threatening, and almost completely lacking in therapeutic benefit.

But it was something, and he felt it wasn't his place to stand between his family and this tiny sliver of hope. Besides, if he dashed away their naïve hopes, then wouldn't he also be killing the tiny hope inside him that just refused to die?

Then they were taking her away. He told her unhearing ears that he loved her. He sat for a long time in the empty room. He wondered if she was still alive, or if maybe everything had worked out. He counted every minute of every hour that he waited.

Close to evening she came back with the only changes in her condition being a large wound and a strong need for more pain relief.

He let out a deep sigh, looked out the window, and continued to grieve for someone who hadn't yet gone.

Searching for Goldfish

Jane Frank

My father has died and I search for goldfish among the water-
lilies—small shocks of orange that might startle the world
out of its disinterest, your harmonies of pale green light,

willows and clouds bouncing from the pond's rose and yellow-
cream surface. I can't see them or feel them on these glossy
pages, so I imagine the water is cold, that they are slow and

sluggish, down deep. Picture you near the end—nine whole
years older than Dad was—your white beard lengthening
each year as you fixate on your aquatic garden. Closer. Soon

the horizon will be gone, and any distinct points: the pink
house with emerald green shutters, the high stone wall, the
ornamental fruit trees. Soon the edges of the pond will be

missing. And then there will only be the illusion of an endless,
harmonious whole. Gardens, light and paint were meditations
for you both: the water darkening and blurring, lilies fusing.

I read somewhere that Giverny fish are grey. That carp and
perch still swim there. Invisible. I dream them gold.

Grave Matters

Marie McMillan

William's death was quick

Our father, her spouse, was gone,
We left, bereft and petrified

Mary Margaret, his wife, our mother,
Spine calligraphed in grieving bent,
Her days in cloistered silence spent,
But, once a week, a trip she made
To yonder cemetery and grave,
Where there she sobbed and spoke to him of
Days long past, of love and trials together,
While planting shrubs and bushes of
Roses, pink and yellow, commemorating
Times long past, once perfumed or thorny

But came the day the granite stone, with
Name and dates, was carved and we all met to
Celebrate its placement on William's head
But his bed could not be found
For Mary Margaret, in her grief,
She had become quite fuddled and had
Numerically confused the final three with two, and for
Long months had spilled her tears o'er grave marked 82,
Where now does rest, from far Xinjiang, a man called
Bolin Zhang

And as we stood 'round 83, humorously and not gravely,
We realised that grief, when shared, is sometimes halved
And laughed, knowing when it fell, not on her beloved's,
But on another's lifeless ears, it only watered roses

Requiescat.

I Promise

Marcia Batton

We found out in February 2018 that the cancer was back. Metastasised. The scans showed it was in two lymph nodes, one in your groin, the other deeper. We had no illusions, you and I; we knew the deeper one was inoperable, a death sentence. Still, to give you your best chance you agreed to surgery.

The surgery was successful in removing the tumour in your groin, but they didn't seal the space completely, so lymph was leaking in. Days of holding your hand while the doctors inserted needles and drained 200ml at a time, hoping your body would seal the gap. But it didn't, and you had to go in for more surgery, on your 62nd wedding anniversary.

I took you to the hospital. While waiting for admission you asked me, 'Why am I here?' It was hard to realise that, as well as the cancer, you were rapidly losing your short-term memory.

They injected you with a blue dye, through a vein in your ankle, so they could see the gap that needed sealing. It left a butterfly tattoo on your inner ankle that faded slowly.

You were so cold when you returned home. It didn't matter how many layers you had on, how hot the room was, I couldn't get you warm.

Mum didn't understand, didn't want to understand, was in complete denial. She kept trying to get you to get up, to do things with her. She was convinced if you would just do some exercise you'd get better.

But we knew it was just time. You had no pain, but everything was an effort. You began to spend your days in bed, hardly eating. I made you home-made chicken broth and fed you, just a cupful a day that, and a scoop of ice-cream was all you wanted and, towards the end, not even that.

I watched you waste away.

We talked; we said all the things we wanted to say to each other. We were lucky. Some people don't get that opportunity, some who get it don't take it and wish they had later when it is too late.

I promised you I would do everything in my power to enable you to die at home, and in no pain. We wrote a letter to mum together, for her to keep and help her through the days when you were gone. I printed it on pretty paper, and you signed it.

When it all got too much, I would leave the room and shed a few tears, but I never let you see.

I nursed you 24/7 through the final days of your life, a privilege. Even then we had laughs and teased each other.

You died peacefully in your sleep January 2019, pain free, in your own home. I kept my promise to you. I treasure that time we had together—some of the hardest days of my life, yet also the best.

My heart aches. I miss you Dad.

Your Mouthguard

Judy Johnson

It was predictable enough
that the couples walking arm in arm
would have multiplied.

And the love scenes in movies
be more frequent than before.

There are more
recipes impossible to downsize from two serves to one:

(a quarter of a pinch
is an eighth of almost nothing.
And how do you measure half an egg, anyway?)

And then there is the mouthguard you once wore
on your upper teeth to protect them
from your nighttime grinding.

How it sits unused on my bedside table in its case.

How I've tried to embrace what we have in common,
(both of us now deprived of your mouth in the dark).

But I can't help coveting
how it holds the indisputable archeology of you;

those tear-shaped indents in their half-moon runnel

where at times, when you clamped down hard in dreams
and broke through the moulded barrier,

pinpricks of light are visible
like some peek-a-boo of a new galaxy
where dentine and thermoplastics
under pressure, give birth
to incisor stars.

But your mouthguard's not Universal.
It's useless for anyone but you.

Devoted forever to the shape of your upper jaw.
A relic, a vessel, a dental record
to identify the dead, that's all.

But despite all the biting, the possession
and the ruin, how much it would have been worth it
to have known you from the inside out
like that.

Negative

Michelle Wright

Eight months after Mum's death, Dad bought a 1967 Leica and turned the laundry into a darkroom. My brother thought it was a positive sign. The first one we'd seen. Until then, during our weekly visits Dad would sit slumped in his recliner, answering our questions in monosyllables; mostly sitting in silence. Now, though, he locked himself away for hours, developing black and white films of the strangers he photographed on his daily walks around the inner-city streets. When he was done, he'd hang the strips of negatives from clothes lines strung across his bedroom. They formed long bars of faces; a curtain we could see through but couldn't cross, like the plastic strips in doorways to keep flies out.

Before we left each Sunday evening, we'd stand in the hallway to say goodbye. He wouldn't answer, but we'd see his face behind the negatives, his eyes straining through the black and silver shapes. He never showed us the finished photographs. In fact, we weren't sure he ever printed them.

His death, unlike Mum's, was sudden. Brain aneurysm. It happened in his sleep. After the funeral, we went to his house every Saturday morning to clear out his belongings, one room at a time. When we got to the laundry, we discovered the undeveloped roll of film sitting by the sink. We thought about having it processed professionally, but after watching a few instruction videos online, we decided to try ourselves. We assembled all the equipment and, in total darkness, transferred the film to the developing tank. With the lights back on we poured the liquids in, one after the other, timing each step, waiting until the process was complete.

When the film was ready, we wiped the excess moisture from the long, thin strip and pegged it up to dry. We didn't recognise the faces right away. It's harder than you'd think on a negative. It was my brother who said, 'That's us.' Thirty-six exposures. Taken from a distance, across the hall, through the half-open bedroom door. Some of us together. Some just my brother or me. Sitting. Standing. Staring into space. Thinking about Mum. Worrying about Dad. Waiting patiently for him to emerge from the dark.

Loss of Faith

Tess Louise

We're too nihilistic to believe in reincarnation
but if we're wrong (and we probably are)
we'll come back as gods
laughing at the ants who speculate about us
and fight over us
with tiny, adorable fists

And Heaven would be so simple
full bookshelves and safe trees
we'll make love to the sound of hymns
never growing tired or sore
and receive prayers like Facebook notifications
that accumulate with every sorry convert

4:15am 30 May 2016

Marian Gordon

There is an oil flare in the desert of my heart
that burns constantly.
Fueled by old forests
the mashed up phenols and tannins
of ancient vegetation.
The empty light
sending sleepless birds
Ricocheting across the skies.

Dusk

Desanka Vukelich

I light the candle and turn on the soft orange lamp. I don't want anything stronger. The blind is up. I like seeing the light change. From my spot on the couch, I can see a little trapezoid of sky. Forming its perimeter are electric wires on one side, the roofline of the workers' cottage the other.

I can only just see the wattlebird bouncing in the branches of the bottlebrush planted into the footpath on my side of the street. It was a good day when I learned the name of that bird, with its cheerful caterwaul. We say hello each morning.

The three variegated trees in the front garden sway gently, as though in a graceful dance, slowing down in time with the dying breeze. I nestle into the cushion behind my head, bring the blanket up over my legs. The candle spits and crackles, releasing its subtle lime fragrance, but mostly beeswax.

Baba and Deda kept bees. Next to the fig tree, just beyond the shade of the treasured oak tree. Do I remember rightly that they were in the full western sun? Can bees withstand direct sunlight?

Their honey was heavy with body and healing properties, just like Baba herself. When I had a sore throat, she'd shove a dessert spoon full of it into my mouth, never asking if I wanted it. I'd wince, my whole face puckering up with the intensity of the moment. The sensation of the spoon too big for my child's mouth, the dense flavour and thick texture of the honey. I hated it, but was too intimidated to protest, other than to let escape whatever small sound I could muster which served as my plea for mercy.

I don't think she ever stopped mourning Deda. I don't remember her wearing colours again. Navy blue. Brown, maybe.

Outside, the neighbour's dog is crying.

What I Hate About Grief

Rhonda Zappelli

I hate the phrase 'taken from us'
It's so passive. Gentle, peaceful even
Belies the violence of fingernail scrapings and bruises
Of ligatures and petechiae.

I hate the word 'spreadeagled'
My high school pocket oxford rendered an image that won't go away
Whenever I catch it unawares
It's a syllabic electroshock device.

I hate the word 'victim'
To be known thereafter as the inconsequence of someone else's actions
Your whole life encapsulated by that, and ours too, as it reverberates and sticks like flypaper
And because naming means becoming, it seeps into the pores and stays forever.

I hate the word 'inquest'
Wooden benches. Paparazzi.
Official. Judicial. Testimonial.
Glacial. Cervical.

I hate the word 'evidence'
It's physical but there's not enough
And what there was, 'they' have lost in the paraffin block of time
The remainder: Circumstantial. Immaterial.

I hate the phrase 'person or persons unknown'
Because I do know those persons in the only way that counts:
The sort of human beings they are:
Decomposing from the inside and filled with the frass of darkness.

But I do love the Sanskrit word 'sanchita'
A form of karma that may deliver justice yet for actions rendered in the past.
I have my fingers crossed.
The only problem is I won't know when to dance on their graves.

Freesias on the Hillside

Hazel Hall

Someone has planted freesias by the trail
to the summit of our hill. They bloom
more profusely since the rains. Perhaps
that is the way of grief—my sudden rush
of childhood memories from the milking shed.
We all chose favourite cows. The faded name
Freesia still remains above the place
where Neil's special beast would reach for feed.
Decades later, after Neil collapsed,
floral perfume drifted with the hymns.
As we left the church I thought I glimpsed
his boyish image near the entourage.
This flood of amaranthine, gold and white
and heavy scent will wrack my sleep tonight.

Sundays

Kathryn Goldie

He rose before dawn. Headed to his spot on the river, just past a bend in the bike path. Set up his bait esky, tackle box, bucket and fold-up stool. A faded hat kept his head warm when it was dark and shaded his face as it grew lighter. He cast and waited, index finger against the line, alert to the slightest touch.

In these quiet, still-dark moments, he loved watching the world blink awake. On the other side of the river, cranes swung into action at the docks. Behind him, cyclists wove between parents and toddlers. Dogs barked as they bounded off-leash. Anything seemed possible.

She would join him when she woke, after the sun had been up an hour or two. If he hadn't caught anything, she'd commiserate and produce a thermos. But usually, as soon as she was there, they started biting. He would stand to play the fish, calling her his good luck charm as he reeled them in – two, three, four.

'My hero!' she would laugh, and beam at him, brighter than the sun. They would walk home, light-hearted, waving to porch-bound neighbours, showing curious kids the catch. He would gut the fish on a table in the yard and she would take them inside, singing, while he scrubbed his hands. He would watch as she prepared the fish, marvelling at the feasts she created: herb-crusted flathead, pan-fried mulloway in lemongrass and chilli, steamed estuary perch with ginger and soy, baked carp with tomatoes and dried limes. Dishes he could never have imagined.

Sundays weren't really about fishing.

Today he sat still and silent. She wouldn't be joining him.

He couldn't bear seeing the life around him now. He tried to block the sound of dogs, bike bells, boats, the laughter of the family of anglers around the bend.

Silent and numb, he shrank the world to the few centimetres of water around his line.

Without his good luck charm, he caught fewer fish. What he did catch, he either threw back or shoved in the freezer for a later he didn't care about. He was no cook, and there was no joy in cooking. No matter what he did, now that she was gone, everything tasted like mud.

In the Sinaai fields

Tineke Van der Eecken

On Saturday mornings even in winter my aunt
scrubbed floors with brown sugar soap while
the top-loader barrel washing machine shook.
She avoided electrocution by wearing wooden clogs.

By midday, Oma's soup was rich with meatballs
and broth from beef bones. She'd scoop
the marrow onto toasts of crustless
white bread, sprinkle salt. Left one for Opa.

On a Sunday morning, years later, his fingers
trembled when he cut a slice of bacon. His fork
scraped eggs in the familiar frying pan. When he
ate, thick veins squirmed on his hands.

Today I cycle through the cobblestone
streets. I find the old farmhouse, now
a building site. The smells of soap and broth
still waft over the Sinaai fields.

Learning to Knit

Olivia Wolfe

I want to learn how to knit.
Firstly, because it is a useful skill.
Secondly, because I see your bald globe and think I could
make a soft home for you. A little less harsh than the one
you already have. I remember my uncle, his skin thinned
and his body not his own. Drained and ballooned
so many times over. I'm ashamed to admit,
I was frightened whenever he came down the stairs.
The sickness wounding his warmth.

Yet I see him sometimes, in people,
sometimes in you. Knit, purl, knit.
80 stitches round. A woollen beanie
isn't comparable to sharing his story.
But it's easier than telling you, leukaemia
laid my uncle in the ground.

My Baby

Jo Skinner

I took a short cut across the oval when a sudden clutch in my pelvis doubled me over, tearing the breath from my throat. I pressed my fist where I imagined the heart to flutter. A fragile red teardrop. When the warm ooze started between my legs, I knew it was over.

A bell shrilled. The squat grey building ejected an uncouth tumble of children who spilled in every direction in a blur of green and grey. So many of them. I crouched in the shade of the enormous tree, the dirt hard beneath my thin soles, the sun fractured through branches and leaves. I pressed hands into my belly even while my baby tore away in painful clots and fragments. A woman hurried past pushing a pram with a crying toddler. Her belly was in full bloom, another one on the way. Bitterness cramped my gut afresh.

I remembered details of that last appointment at the clinic. Ray sitting on the edge of his chair, elbows on knees, eyes to the floor. He was suspicious of medical procedures. I'd promised him we would stop trying after I turned forty. But then the date passed and there were all those women still having babies at forty-one, forty-two and older.

'It is hard to be optimistic about your chance of success.'

The doctor had been so business like, the magnetic white board behind him crowded with photographs of babies. The success stories. 'Perhaps you would consider egg donation?'

Ray had looked up then, drawn the line. 'Thanks, but no.'

I forced myself to sit very still, clamping my lips tight. Ray hated a scene. The doctor leant back in his chair folded his arms. 'You have one embryo left. It's not the best quality. How about we give it a go?'

I suppressed my initial outrage. How dare he suggest it was poor quality. It was not just a collection of cells but a baby, our baby. I pictured myself wheeling one of those huge prams into The Coffee Spot, complaining about sleepless nights and cracked nipples with the others while gazing down on curled fists, lashes brushing soft cheeks.

Another cramp gripped me, made me cry out. The stream of children had thinned to a trickle. The bark was rough through flimsy cotton along my vertebrae. My insides were hot and raw. In that moment, I longed to curl inside Ray's arms again, to feel his warm breath against my cheek. How long since we had shared skin to skin intimacy? My throat constricted with fresh regret at the unease that now stretched taut between us. A breeze shifted the leaves, light gathered and retreated. A spider clung precarious, spread eagled on its torn web above my head.

I wept at the senseless order of things and walked home, the red stain of my losses and grief splattered across the back of my dress.

Three Bora Rings Lost to a Highway Bypass

Kate Olivieri

This is not so many
In the whole country, never given
All that blood taken.

But I would not do it, myself. No.

A meeting place

Travelling in time
How do we remember them?
Important place to go.

You did not use it, yourself, so – how would you know?

With every new small loss

Country loses itself more.
Again, again, again
This lore makes it so.

Cars will drive over them now, below

Sun, rain, wind, dark, light

Trees, vines, bracken and branch
Cover the bora rings and go
Leave the ancestors alone.

They did not do it themselves. And now, you know.

Revelations

Pieta Morello

We meet at the cemetery now. We used to meet in cafés and talk for hours over coffees. We used to go to pubs and restaurants for dinner and away for weekends. We used to talk every week, and more often if there were crises—poor exam results, the basketball trials, the dramas of teenage boys and helicopter Mums. We used to laugh all the time as we had the same quirky sense of humour. We had good beautiful boys and we were untouchable.

We talk about different things now: PTSD, psychiatrists, coroner reports and other unthinkable topics. There are always tears now. I feel like I am made of water. I am crying rivers. I am the Nile, the Mississippi, the Amazon ... all the big ones! It's like I have a thin frozen surface with a raging river of tears underneath. How is your son? How are you? How is your friend? All questions which breach the surface.

I am struggling to describe the depths of our grief in words. Heartbroken, broken, in pieces, in pain ... are just not accurate enough. I find that people don't really want to know how bad it is. They are being polite and want to acknowledge the loss. Suddenly I am a snivelling mess and through the tears I am saying, 'I'm actually OK. No, really I am.' Unsurprisingly, they don't believe me, but are horrified at the reaction they have prompted. Socially, it's proving awkward.

I am shocked at the fallout from his death. The ongoing repercussions, people's judgemental opinions, the guilt, the triggers, all take me by surprise. I am surprised by the community at the cemetery, what friends do and what friends don't do. Strangers' compassion. I am doing things I never imagined. On anniversaries I place flower bouquets and candles where they don't really belong—in a public place, in front of strangers. I see a grief counsellor. I attend a 21st gathering at a gravesite without the beloved guest of honour. I cry in the car and in the middle of the night. I know the best time to put grass on a grave. It is another world.

I am a big talker but I am very careful with my words now. I am tiptoeing and every single word is considered. I do not mention my son unless my friend does. In response to her question, I just tell her he is OK. That is all she wants to hear. She does not have room for him in her pain just yet. I don't tell her that he has graduated from university, he had a 21st party, he cries in the shower, he's playing his sad playlist today. She would not be able to bear it. I have learned the power of words. *Are you OK?* is off the table as I know she is not. I will do anything to help keep her upright. I don't mind. I still have my son.

Gravel Road Wail

Rachel Baxter

You structured your death,
scheduled, precise.
Choosing your gift-box like a joker,
the forecast for the parade.
Twenty-eight degrees,
an ice-cream van out the front.
Blueberry Heaven.
A wafer cone
points to the dirt.
Salty aqua splashes on my white canvas shoes.

I was driving a month later,
on old country bends.
A large sound came up and out,
like a faulty siren.
Grief in stereo.
On the side of the road, I stared at the intricate gravel,
my head low, counting the pebbles in four-four time.
Despairing.
Amazed.
I had volume,
baying at the trees, the careless universe.

In the city, I take the train.
Reading a book too close to my face.
Breathing through my feet,
or the top of my head.

A man with a crossword
asks me to spell monocle.
M-O-N-O-C-L-E,
I think.
I am grateful for this interlude.
Who knows when the gravel-road wail might come?
Uncensored.
Thunderous.
And there are no pebbles here to count.
The next station is *Glenferrie.*

The Goodest Boy

Helena Spyrou

Little Dubby
ears, alert, set a little too far apart
eyes, kohl rimmed, dart from stick to me
to stick, to me, to stick.

Quick to sniff out a stray ball and leap to its rescue
as it escapes the swing of a young boy playing tennis.

A soccer ball too big
for your mouth to carry?
You'll give it a go, again
and again, and again.

Your tail antenna dances with grasses
and signals your hidey holes when I lose sight of you.

You've no stop button
little Dubby
but in a COVID stage four slow down
your pace changes too.

Is it hard for you to wait, curled in the front seat
your russet colours dimming?

Together we watch twilight turn to night
and in a long still while
the nurse comes and I drive home
leaving you in ICU.

I sleep, I wake – force breath in.
I sleep, I wake – look for you.

In the morning, I call your second mother.
The two of us are with you now
while you surrender
as Socrates did to hemlock.

We stroke your ears, set a little too far apart.
and they fall against your kohl rimmed eyes.

You were the goodest boy
tuned in to the goodest core of us.

My Last Swim With My Father

Helena Pastor

The night before my father's funeral, my brother got very drunk. He played songs from the past, trying to work out appropriate music for the funeral. I stayed in the spare room, writing my father's eulogy. At one stage, when I went into the kitchen for a glass of water, I found my brother dancing around the room to *Spirit in the Sky* while my mother sat nearby, shell-shocked, like a victim of war. My sister was encouraging my brother to release his grief through the music.

The next day we went to my father's funeral at the crematorium in Nerang, where I delivered the eulogy. Only ten people attended my father's funeral because my mother wanted it that way. I didn't agree with her decision. My father was a successful migrant, a Gold Coast Bridge champion, a former Olympic boxer —I thought he deserved more. Meanwhile, nearly a thousand kilometres away at Berry on the south coast of New South Wales, my oldest brother wept as he recovered from a knee replacement.

A month later, we had a family celebration of my father's life in Berry. On the first night, I'd booked a table at the local pub for all of us and I was furious because the fellow who had taken the booking—someone I had gone to school with—had spelled our name wrong. *For fuck's sake*, I thought, *we lived in this town for so many years and you can't remember our fucking name?* I was angry at everything. The following day we went to Seven Mile Beach and walked down to the sea with my father's ashes. I remember the kids running down to the water and it was cold and windy. Our hair and clothes were blowing everywhere, and the skirt I was wearing kept blowing up. I saw my brother's wife walking down to the beach with irises in her hands, and it suddenly hit me what we were there for—this was death, the death of someone in our family.

As we stood in a semi-circle near the shoreline, my oldest brother gave a speech. Then, we all waded into the sea, scattering the ashes and the flowers into the water. It felt right to release my father into the sea. After the last of the ashes were gone, people started walking away. But I stayed on the shore. I was going for a swim, even though it was winter, the end of June, the wind freezing cold. I stripped off to my bra and undies and went into the water where we had thrown the ashes and the blue irises. I was so cold I thought my heart would stop beating. I stood for a minute or two, thinking about my father. About all the swims and beach experiences we'd had together, all the sandcastles he'd made for me. Then I went under.

The Theft

Richenda Rudman

Someone said
somewhere on a screen
that a small green car had been taken from the grave of a son.

A photo was published: one small green car nestled in a round-fingered grip,
the shine of spittle on its little wheels;
the lime doors in the hug of flannelette.

Viewers' rage cackled full wattage:
stories thrown like logs on to a fire;
stories of desecration, of stolen flowers and dolls and books.

Some denied the despicability of the act,
suggesting a storm took it,
suggesting concealment—a chance spraying of dirt by gravedigger.

Some asked questions:
what section of the graveyard?
(As if thieving favoured one denomination!)

Some solutions sought to offer balm:
Why not weave flowers, dolls and cars through chicken wire?
(As if being stunned on a fence would make it harder for the lowlifes!)

Headstone words for a short sweet life stayed
under clouds being carried by the sky,
but nothing returned a small green car

or the grip of a small son.

They Arrived Sleeping

Maree Gardner Chapman

Both of them arrived sleeping. There was no-one by the bedside, no-one to explain or console in those days. It was all routine. Would this ever heal? Hard to grasp. Grief fell to that soft place in the abyss of the heart. It hid there. Crept out in the dead of night or the cold light of day. Like a gentle breeze or a thunder storm that pounded the psyche. Changed it forever. Time did make it easier. However, triggers remained the enemy.

In the midst of it all came opportunity to nurture somewhere else. Gifts of tiny hands and feet, warm snuggles and the smell of powdered skin. Grief softened by generous women.

Side by Side

Michelle Brock

In those early days when you were a fresh-faced architect and I was a student
from the tropics, week by week, more than a thousand miles apart,
love letters wove the threads between us …

blossoms twirl
their petal petticoats
springtime
the blush and quiver
of young love

As soon as I graduated, I headed south and we set up house.
You skited that you'd make old bones but three daughters
and ten years later, you became a victim of genetics
and wrote your final letter …

I flick
a smooth black stone
across the water
one … two … three skips
and it's gone

I never felt you deserted me, you simply stepped aside
to let me finish what we'd started …

thirty years on
a flicker of you
in the eyes
of the grandchild
you'll never know

Some days your empty chair casts a shadow across the floor and
I try to imagine a parallel life with you. In a box on the top shelf
of my wardrobe, I still have all our love letters …

a magpie
hovers above its song
wings outstretched …
teach me to relinquish
the things I cannot hold

Is joy a better teacher than sorrow or do they each, stand stronger, side by side?

A Stone to Remember

Deb Sestak

We have been in the cemetery for close to an hour climbing over broken tombstones, fallen trees, and tangled ivy. There is a damp, earthy smell and the air is crisp. My feet sink into seventy years of leaf litter and I wonder if it's possible to disappear into a sinkhole in this overgrown and unloved graveyard.

We are searching for our grandmother's grave. She died 86 years ago. She was 42 years old. Dad was five. We are here to place a stone on her grave, to remember and honour her, for dad and for ourselves.

This day has been a long time coming. Dad never returned to Poland after he escaped in 1948. He visited Europe many times but never Poland. None of us have ever visited Poland. While Dad was alive it felt too hard. Too hard to plan and get excited about. Too hard for him to share the stories that brought him so much pain and too hard for us to hear them.

Finding the grave is difficult. We spread out and try a strategic approach. We have the grave location—sector, row, number—but the row markers are long gone, and this place is vast and dark. The early autumn sun merely peeps through the dense canopy of trees and the sound of our footsteps are deadened by the soft, deep mulch. We lose sight of each other and call out every so often to keep track of where we are.

I see that Mum is searching on her own and move towards her. And then my sister sings out, 'I've found it.'

The headstone we find is on the ground, green from damp, toppled by a tree. We sit in silence on the log seat created by the tree, each in our own thoughts of dad, his story, our history. We don't share our thoughts—it's hard to speak. I want to say something to break the intensity, to laugh instead of cry. I keep quiet. This is a profound moment, our first tangible connection with dad's past. This is the place where he stood as a young boy and shed tears for his dead mama.

I imagine the family standing together weeping for their loss while they recite the mourner's *kaddish*. I see the coffin lowered into the ground, the shovel erect in the mound of dirt beside the grave and the men in the family standing in silence, waiting their turn to help bury their wife, mother, sister, as their last act of respect and devotion.

One by one we each place the stones, brought with us from the other side of the world, onto the remains of her grave. Slowly we retrace our steps back along the main boulevard to the cemetery gates and the modern world.

Leaves on a Stream

Mitchell Welch

Light a candle, or have a candle ready
To light at the right moment.

Intolerable hours hold each other's wakes
and we hold on waiting for this last loss
to feel like something we might begin to grasp.

Picturing ourselves looking down from above
we look down sitting with heads bowed
cold hands clapped in hopeless laps waiting
to play our parts in the closed-circuit telecast.

Quasi-Proto-Indo-European feelings creep in
like dread of death in a cave bear's cave
to trap our breaths in the depths of our heads.

There's nothing to be said. Death lives here
and the still life hanging on the wall is dead.

Time passes in the kitchen sucking in its breath
to keep from breathing in the reek.

The screen flickers like the flick of a tongue
that wants to speak, to say 'Don't look away'.

There's nothing else. The image-stream
lights up in horizontal bars and there's the Father
shuffling his palm cards. There's the screen
behind the cardboard casket for the slideshow.

The widow, the mother, two adult children, a brother.

Looking through the gap between the feeling
and the seeing, the seeing and the being there
for real feels like the ceiling in the kitchen caving in.

The first grave I reckon was a sealed cave.
A crumbled limestone dome, the first catacomb.

I have my candle. Tell me when it's time.

Still Point

Anahata Giri

Your grief touches my grief and our lives hold hands for a moment.

My first baby. The ultrasound at 13 weeks.
The device cold moves over my skin, looking in.
Her arm extends from her blue uniform and sweeps across,
smooth then stops, sudden, then quicker, the rhythm is wrong - she is searching.
I stare at her dead pan face and something in me goes cold.
I know before she brings the doctor in.

He says: A simple procedure. It's Friday afternoon so right now, before the weekend.
What if I birth her? I ask in my ignorance.
We cannot guarantee the safety of that and we do not recommend it, he says.

But something in me says wait. I carry her home and phone a midwife.
She gives me the sacred knowledge and the practical.
She says: it will feel like bad period pain. Use a thermometer.
If you have a fever go to the hospital. Otherwise you are safe, your body knows what to do.
She says: birthing her will help with the grief.

Then the ache, the tears and the contractions begin and I know it's the rhythm the body needs.

Your story. The doctor told you: the limbs, the organs, the cells -
twisted impossibility - so you name her and carry her across nine months,
across the terrain of love and grief.

They said: why not finish it with a clinical nip in the bud? Why go through all that?

But go through you did and you birthed your wee babe with the courage of a mother, with a love beyond impossible.
Born still. A moment poised becomes the still point in your heart.
It was their words, harsh, that sent you home to Ireland to grieve,
to be wrapped in a circle of women you know,
to create a sacred boundary around the sanctity of your beautiful choice.

I carried the knowledge a few days. You, for months.
We carry the lost babies as we go on to birth four children between us.

Loss whispers in the rustle of leaves, in the receding tide.
The still point becomes the fulcrum, tipping toward life.
Grief is the bridge between death and hope.

We say:
We know how to birth beauty,
We know how to birth the sacred.
We know how to birth the world.

Hope

Chloe Warren

Sometimes I feel I may as well peel my own skin from the bone to try and make a new life without you.

One Friday, you took the day off work and we drove around the city looking in second-hand stores. I was collecting green glass and you came to me, so proud, with a lime green vase. I didn't want you to know it was the wrong shade, the wrong clarity; I just wanted to meet your pride so I bought it anyway. You always loved the odd glazes, the drizzles, the imperfect ceramics.

As we crouched in front of glass cabinets, dusty carpets making our throats tingle and eyes itch, our worlds shrank together and I inhaled your whispers, let them dance on my skin. Between tightly packed shelves, overburdened with plastic toys, cheap jewellery, and mismatched crockery, I stole kisses and knew what love felt like.

I bought you a vase once. Soft pinks swirled into mint green, smooth and rounded: it looked so quiet and warm that it reminded me of you. Climbing into your car outside my house, I told you I'd bought you a present. 'Is it you?' you asked, drinking me in.

We took art classes together, as equally enamoured with our ideas of each other as we were of ideas of our creative selves. We brought each other traces of who we wanted to be and helped each other up, so proud, so open, so in love.

You brought me a book entitled, *You are an Artist*. I was your artist.

Now not only do I see you in every vase, but I see you in my own hands and heart whenever I dream up something beautiful to give to the world. Ceramics make my heart hurt.

I worry that the parts of me you loved have dissolved since you left. I worry that all the things you nurtured have shrunk away from me in bitterness. I worry that there is nothing left of me to love because I give nothing away.

When we bring children into the world, we present it to them as a perfect balance of rejection and acceptance. 'Protect yourself, but know that you are safe and loved,' we tell them, as though that makes sense.

You got lost along the way and now the only way you can feel safe is without love: you have nothing to lose and nothing to fear. What I would give to unpick it all and stitch it up with us.

My psychologist told me that you left because 'fear trumps love,' and I don't know how to go on trying now I realise that is true.

We lie to our children about the balance of love and grief so that we can bury our useless hope elsewhere, so we do not have to look it directly in the eye, and so it is not our responsibility to hold it.

I cannot hold it.

Inappropriate Widow

Elizabeth Clarke

Today I took his will to the Supreme Court,
to lodge probate.
That's it, I thought, That's it done.
The list of jobs.
Undertaker
Funeral
Playlist
Wake
Death certificate
Wills found
Copies, Copies of everything
Affidavits signed
Ashes collected in a blue plastic urn that could be mistaken for washing powder.
Petition for probate lodged.
Its been six weeks and three days.
Its not quite over, still the goddam tax return and house sale to sort.
Twenty-two adventurous years together.
Two children,
four countries,
six homes.
All wrapped up with one black ribbon in six weeks and three days.
I feel faintly ridiculous as well as sad; a sympathy card moonlighting as a bookmark makes my eyes sting. I am shrouded in black, the result of a lazy wardrobe rather than widows honour.
Like my mother, the catharsis of a good cry escapes me. We became widows in the same week.
Unlike her, I don't worry about it, except to wonder if I'm a psychopath.
Am I numb?
Do I not feel the pain?
I don't know.

It makes me feel like an inappropriate widow.

Not just because of my dark humour. Who else drinks G&T whilst laying out their husbands body? Smearing a taste across his lips so he isn't left out. Then kissing them for the last time and

sprinkling sand on his toes as we say our final farewell.

Waiting

Denise O'Hagan

I reach for the comb, mindful of the drag of rounded teeth across skin as translucent as tracing paper. My hands are the latest in a long line of hands that have tended that hair, and here in this final frame I recall what I never knew, the soft movement of a small hairbrush over a baby's head. Now her hair is feathery and light again, and makes such an imperceptible impression on the skull beneath that the comb becomes nothing more than an instrument of delicate rearrangement. I'm pleased with my efforts: she wears her hair like a nightcap, draping down past the globe of her still plump ear lobe and over the play of ridges at her collarbone. The honeyed light from the window behind her flares for a moment on a strand of auburn, or is it a trick of the light? Her physical casing is receding before me, and I become aware of something else emerging; I know that in tending my mother I am tending her spirit. She is neat, patient, waiting. I wait with her.

Day's Eye

Kate O'Neil

for Jennifer
The daisy's petals open in the morning to show the central yellow disc, and close over it in the evening.

On that heatwave day in the school chapel,
windows open for relief from a slight breeze,
the room was bright with yellow:

yellow for happiness, hope, promise –
your favourite colour –
in roses, daisies, marigolds, sunflowers.

Your friends and family wore yellow,
affirming the light you were,
and not the dark of their grief.

Kendall described the raised eyebrows
at the funeral parlour: 'Yellow?'
'Yes, and her cows will be there.'

The cows, placed among the flowers,
were as innocent of their loss
as the yellow summer air.

Your favourite, a little threadbare,
alone on the end of your coffin,
stared at a daisy

At Twenty-four

Bron Bateman

I did not even know how much I wanted
a son until he was born.
Girls were easy, and I had two of them,
but he would make me a woman.
Down's Syndrome they said. *Heart defects.*

All I wanted to do was take him home
and rock him, safe.
I would show them all, I thought, as I
whispered impossible things in his ear,
a life spread out like a map before us,
with mazes and cul-de-sacs
where a child could play in safety.

This would be our story.

But one December morning
his heart exploded in his chest
and not even the best doctor in the country
could knit it back together.

They took me to view his body on the bed.
Dressed in a sky-blue, Bonds growsuit.
So small
and still.

All I remember doing after that was cupping my hands
around my eyes, pressing my face against the window,
surveying the grass and road below

with forensic precision. Carefully licking
the glass my nose was pressed against,
dust and grit on my tongue, acrid and bitter.
Grains of sand and fine dust coating my mouth.
Much later I learnt from mythology that
this is how clay becomes flesh:
dust and grit mixed with saliva,
A creature brought forth from pulverised stone.

My very own Golem.

The Road Home

R I Quin

What day is it?
I lose track.
Linear time coagulates,
clotting as converging lines across a floor.
Days merge.
Consummation by osmosis is complete.
We are the hospital.
We breathe with it, swallow it,
drink it in, sleep with, wake with it.

The outside world is myth.
Glimpsed.
A breath of wind against a curtain,
filtered sunlight, traffic passing.
Less plausible
than clocks and seconds,
than tablets, temperatures, needles,
networks connecting life via veins
to bags on hooks.

We could leave through automatic doors,
consume real air.
Re-join the world.
Reverse out, turn left, slip into position,
stop at lights, stare ahead, radio spewing out tunes.
Be at home,
but not the same home.
An empty house
waiting to be reshaped.

Index of Stories and Poems

www.ingramcontent.com/pod-product-compliance
Lightning Source LLC
Chambersburg PA
CBHW020640130726
47903CB00003BA/927
* 9 7 8 0 6 4 8 8 5 0 4 5 8 *